KUNG-FU MONTHLY

THE ARCHIVE SERIES

BRUCE LEE IN ACTION

BY THE EDITORS OF
KUNG-FU MONTHLY

COMPILED AND EDITED BY
CARL FOX

PIT WHEEL PRESS
BARNSLEY

Published by
PIT WHEEL PRESS LIMITED
www.pitwheelpress.com

Copyright © 2023 Pit Wheel Press Limited. All Right Reserved. No part of this book may be reproduced, scanned or distributed in any printed or electronic form without permission.

BRUCE LEE IN ACTION

Copyright © 1977 by H. Bunch Associates Ltd. (except where copyright on certain photographic material already exists). This publication or any parts thereof may not be reproduced in any form whatsoever without permission in writing from the copyright proprietor.

A Pit Wheel Press edition, published by special arrangement with Dennis Publishing, London.

First Printing 1977
Revised Edition 2023

Printed in the United Kingdom
ISBN 978-1-915414-11-3

BRUCE LEE is a trademark of Bruce Lee Enterprises, LLC.

DEDICATED TO

MICK AND LYNN PADGETT
OF *THE BARNSLEY SHOTOKAN KARATE CLUB*

MY FIRST TEACHERS IN THE
ART OF THE EMPTY HAND

"Only on certain occasion will one repeat a kata a number of times - and that is for mental and spiritual purposes - to force you to go beyond the body, the mind and the art. You have to live the kata. Use all your power as if in life or death."

Keinosuke Enoeda
(1935-2003)

ACKNOWLEDGEMENTS

I would like to thank the following people for their help and participation in the making of this book:

James Bishop
Andrew Kimura
John Little

John Overall
Carlotta Serantoni
Chris Thompson

Special Thanks
Martin O'Neill

CREDITS

Original 1977 Edition

PHOTO CREDITS
Golden Harvest Films, Warner Bros Films
& Chester Maydole

The Kung-Fu Monthly Archive Series

Research, Editing, Layout & Design
Carl Fox

Editorial Assistance
George Fox

Photograph Acknowlegements
Kung-Fu Monthly & Carl Fox

Kung-Fu Monthly Collage Image
Copyright © 2023 Carl Fox

KUNG-FU
MONTHLY

THE ARCHIVE SERIES
BRUCE LEE IN ACTION
CHAPTERS

ABOUT THE KFM ARCHIVE SERIES   11

FOREWORD (2023)   13

INTRODUCTION (1977)   21
In just a few short years, Bruce Lee turned the glory of martial combat into compulsive cinema viewing the whole world over...

01   THE BIRTH OF THE BRUCE LEE LEGEND   31
Precision with Power - A Kung Fu System Tailor-made for Trouble - The Hong Kong Connection - A Way Out of the 'Classical Mess' - The Little Dragon Makes Enemies.

02   SO I SAID, "THE HELL WITH IT!"   49
The Little Dragon Transfers to New Locations - Hollywood Grabs the Powerhouse Genius - The World Studies New Tactics of Death - The Censorship Problem - Bruce Lee's Supreme Skill at Last Recognised.

03   THE VIOLENCE OF BRUCE LEE   71
The Hong Kong Press Lashes Out - Misjudgements, Prejudice and Hasty Conclusions - Even the Facts Sometimes are Wrong - The Little Dragon Sails on Regardless - His Fighting Fury Cannot be Abated.

04   THE LESSONS OF JEET KUNE DO   85
Speed, Power, Agility and Knowledge - The Mighty Tools of Bruce Lee's Trade - The Net Widens, the Word Spreads - Developing the Fighting Instinct - Asia's Number One Son Teaches the Possibilities of Spiritually Guided Combat - Though the Master is Gone, the Legacy He Left Remains with Us.

KUNG-FU MONTHLY

THE ARCHIVE SERIES
ABOUT THE SERIES

Kung-Fu Monthly is a name synonymous with Bruce Lee, not only in the United Kingdom but throughout the world. It is a legend in its own right and a brand immediately recognisable by not only the font but also the famous "flying man" logo.

The popularity of the magazine at the peak of the Kung Fu Craze in the 1970s was unrivalled and its success was almost entirely down to pure luck.

Legend has it that *Kung-Fu Monthly* began life as a gamble by underground comic book publisher Felix Dennis after questioning a queue of kids outside a Soho cinema, waiting to see *Enter the Dragon* in early 1974. On paper, the idea seemed to serve the then-current trend of Bruce Lee and was deemed to have a shelf life of three to six months but a year after its launch, *Kung-Fu Monthly* had become the biggest-selling Bruce Lee magazine in the world.

After the demise of the Official Bruce Lee Fan Club in 1976, *Kung-Fu Monthly* launched their own. The KFM Bruce Lee Society ran for thirty quarterly newsletters from 1976 to 1983 and at the time of closing, had seen over five thousand eager Bruce Lee fans become members throughout its tenure, with the formidable Pam Hadden at the forefront throughout its seven active years.

Kung-Fu Monthly and The Bruce Lee Society were jointly responsible for the UK's first Bruce Lee Convention held on May 19th 1979 and the first Bruce Lee Film Festival held on December 1st 1979.

Kung-Fu Monthly and later *Personal Computer World*, had turned H. Bunch Associates from an underground publisher on the verge of bankruptcy to a publishing powerhouse, eventually becoming Dennis Publishing, named after its founder, Felix Dennis.

That leads us to today.

In February 2021, I approached Dennis Publishing with an idea for a project that I'd thought of doing for many years - scan, convert, edit and compile all seventy-nine issues of the iconic *Kung-Fu Monthly* magazine into book form, in order to present it to a new audience, as well as preserve its place in history.

It was the longest-running dedicated Bruce Lee magazine of its kind anywhere in the world (by frequency and circulation) and I wanted to pay homage to that. Such was its success and popularity that it was licensed throughout the world; in fourteen countries and in eleven languages. That doesn't even take into account the non-official bootlegs which appeared in China and Turkey. Nothing has matched it before or since. It truly has stood the test of time and having done so, has reached legendary status.

Kung-Fu Monthly is a snapshot of a time long gone; a time which the original fans remember with fondness and a time which new fans will hopefully discover.

The *Kung-Fu Monthly Archive Series* is dedicated to Felix Dennis and everyone associated with the magazine; not just the staff but also the fans, who would buy copies of the magazines in their millions over its lifetime and help cement the publication's place in British Pop Culture history.

Special thanks must also go to Carlotta Serantoni at Dennis Publishing for her assistance in allowing this project to go ahead.

Carl Fox
February 2022

KUNG-FU MONTHLY

THE ARCHIVE SERIES
BRUCE LEE IN ACTION

FOREWORD

UNDERSTANDING JEET KUNE DO

Bruce Lee's electrifying presence, movies, books, and philosophy continue to inspire people, especially young men from all over the word. He was a renaissance man with a creative mind, a researcher, thinker, innovator and a fanatical physical trainer.

Bruce Lee grew from being a rather ordinary young teenager, a "wiseguy", and street fighter into someone very special. He overcame stumbling blocks and obstacles in his life that would have crushed most people. He reinvented himself through sheer hard work and determination and used his mind creatively to become the most famous martial artist of his generation. The martial art that he created, "Jeet Kune Do," has its own principles, philosophy, history and technical skills, giving it a unique approach. Rather than blindly following others, Lee wanted to create a unique scientific and rational approach to martial ways and the fighting arts.

Jeet Kune Do has its own training and development methods using the base art of Jun Fan Gung Fu (Jun Fan method) which can be traced back to Wing Tzun and Grand Master Ip Man in Hong Kong and the early 1960s in Seattle USA. It cannot be categorised as a "Chinese" or an "American" martial art. It owes a great debt in its evolution to the brilliant martial art of Wing Tzun and to his teacher Grandmaster Ip Man, who influenced Bruce a great deal in terms of creative thinking and combat approaches. Jeet Kune Do uses Western boxing skills and methods and western fencing theory, and Lee was developing his approach to grappling before his untimely death. Bruce Lee did not completely abandon his Jun Fan method but integrated the core principles throughout his martial arts development from Grand Master Ip Man, to the Seattle Jun Fan Gung Fu Institute established in 1963 under Sigung Taky Kimura, Oakland Jun Fan Gung Fu Institute under Sifu James Lee and the Jun Fan Gung Fu Institute Los Angeles 1967 under Sifu Dan Inosanto. This where he created Jeet Kune Do as freedom of expression in both thinking, training and in fighting methodology. Using anything that works, "Consider all ways, but being bound by none" was his watchword.

Jeet Kune Do is a rational martial art and looks towards our capacity to think, reason, and seek the truth, both in combat and in life and is a process of constant refinement. Bruce Lee wanted to break people away from dead set patterns and have a modern scientific approach to test and evaluate against a resisting opponent who was really trying to hit and hurt you. Drilling realistically and sparring was the crucible for testing if something had value and was worth studying. Using appropriate essential skills are paramount with proper training time, using stand-up and ground fighting with and without weapons. The techniques used are harmonious and skilled movements; taking small steps forward each day is vital. The focus is on mechanics - not just hitting numbers of repetitions. Doing 500 kicks per day or 500 armbars may not make you any better, as you need to emphasise the feeling and skilled mechanics of the movements. Building your individual knowledge and skill sets are vital to making real improvement. There is no big bang in Jeet Kune Do. The mindset is not exceptional; it's just regarded as another day to develop calmness under pressure and to enhance mental discipline. Lee was a fanatical physical trainer and worked out every day.

However, Bruce Lee did not randomly or constantly add other martial arts techniques or styles and was careful and discerning about doing so. He liked to scientifically test an idea before he would consider adopting it. Much was discarded by him during testing.

Jeet Kune Do is both an art and a science to give you a strategic tactical and mechanical advantage, as knowledge builds skills, not mindless or random drilling. Any movement that does not improve skills is considered to be a waste of time, and time is precious.

The technical basis of Jeet Kune Do has not changed that much and includes the following:

- *On-Guard Position*
- *Footwork and Mobility*
- *Punching and Kicking*
- *Five Ways of Attack*
- *Economy of Motion*
- *Interception*
- *Energy and Sensitivity Drills*
- *Learning to Fight in all Ranges*

Thinking fast is also emphasised by Lee as it can give you the edge in life and in battle. Emphasis is placed upon aerobic fitness and flexibility and being dynamic and strong without looking like a body builder.

"I favour moving like a boxer. Jeet Kune Do offers more freedom, more self-expression."

"It is as I practice it, more offensive than defensive. At the moment of attack, you intercept the attack and attack in return; it's alive, it's free."

- Bruce Lee

Bruce Lee is credited with saying "Research your own experiences. Absorb what is useful. Reject what is useless. And add what is essentially your own." However, apparently there is no evidence of that quote in his personal papers or recordings.

He did advise, "Shun what is trivial and discard what is ornamental." It is not daily increase but daily decrease.

Jeet Kune Do eventually became, "The Way of No Way," with no restrictions or limits, with complete freedom of expression; a mirror to examine and improve ourselves emotionally and physically.

Martin O'Neill
The Jeet Kune Do Mindset

Sources: *Tao of Jeet Kune Do* by Bruce Lee and *Bruce Lee: A Warriors Journey* by John Little

KUNG-FU
MONTHLY

THE ARCHIVE SERIES
BRUCE LEE
IN ACTION

KUNG-FU MONTHLY

THE ARCHIVE SERIES
BRUCE LEE IN ACTION
INTRODUCTION (1977)

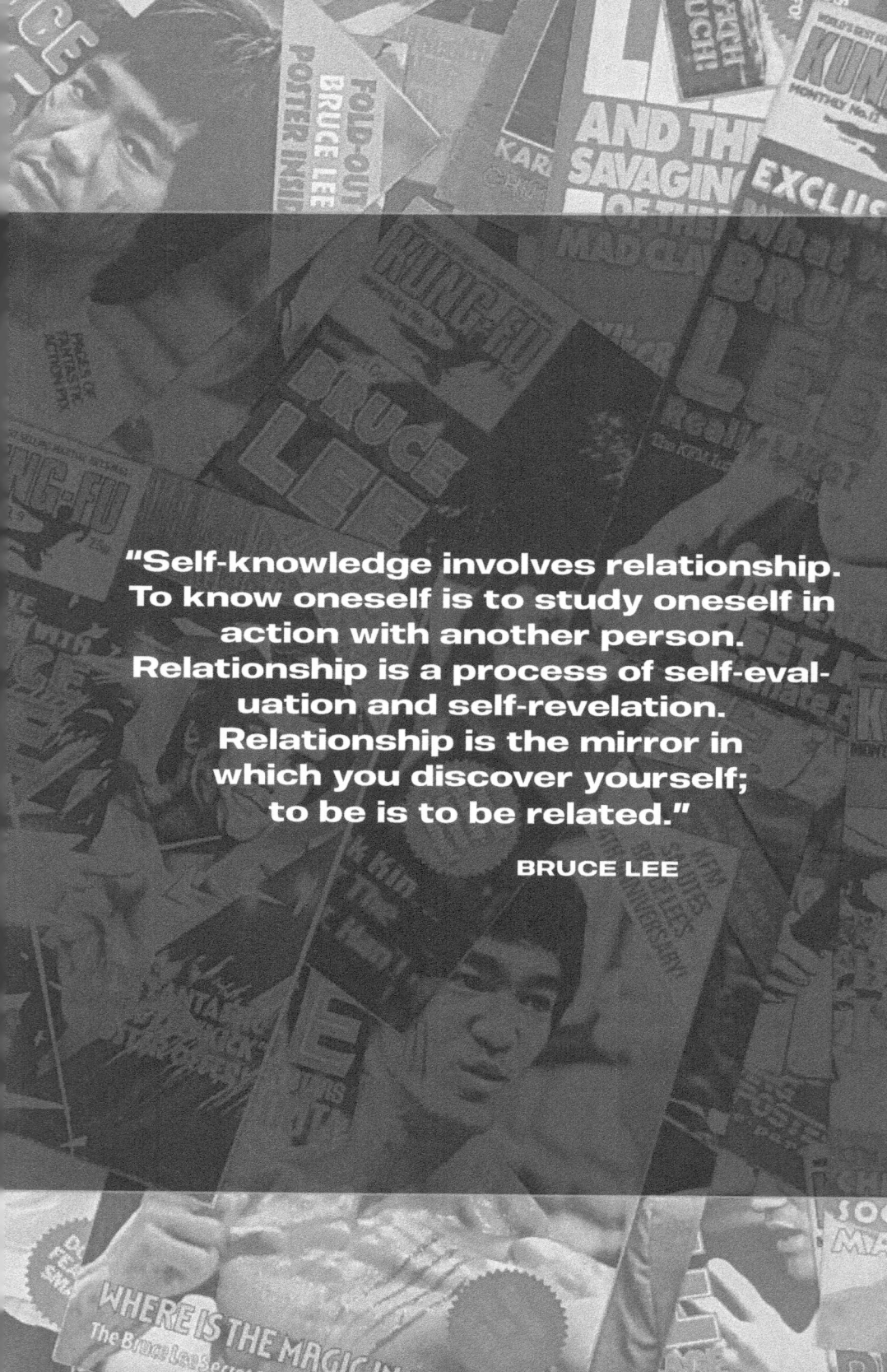

"Self-knowledge involves relationship. To know oneself is to study oneself in action with another person. Relationship is a process of self-evaluation and self-revelation. Relationship is the mirror in which you discover yourself; to be is to be related."

— BRUCE LEE

It took just four major films for Bruce Lee to brilliantly transfer the glory of martial combat into compulsive cinema viewing the whole world over. Now, once again, the editors of *Kung-Fu Monthly* salute this unforgettable achievement with an historic new publication. Over the last few years, many a unique milestone has been passed in the never-ending search to find the truth behind the greatest Kung Fu artist ever known. Now, as a fitting sequel to *The Secret Art of Bruce Lee*, they proudly offer *Bruce Lee in Action*.

This new book carries a veritable plethora of fine pictures of Bruce Lee in full fighting fury - many entirely new to readers. And, better news still, there's also been added some more instructional gems from Chester Maydole's fabulous set of never-before-seen Lee training pictures. These again are accompanied by sharply explicit, move-by-move explanatory captions, excellently penned for the book by Paul Simmons. There can be no doubt that *Bruce Lee in Action* represents an invaluable addition to the available range of books, biographies and manuals on Lee and the techniques of Jeet Kune Do.

As educational aids, the new pictures are of tremendous interest - as indicators of the way Bruce Lee lived, worked and trained, they are beyond price. Lee built his world around action. Whether as a street fighter, a martial artist supreme, or a screen superstar, his approach was always consistent - almost to a fault. Action equals results.
Nothing, he believed, could be achieved by thought or good intention alone. Naturally, much of the time, this 'action' manifested itself in the form of fighting - whether for real or otherwise - and in this book, every avenue of action is painstakingly followed and explored.

The scope of the subject is understandably vast, and quotes, anecdotes, facts, half-truths and sometimes even downright lies continue to flow by the door in an endless stream. The book's task - to select and report on the most important - has not been an easy one. A point most certainly deserving of inclusion has been the so-called 'morality' aspect. Should the Master's films be taken simply as a unique combination of art and entertainment or, as some will insist, do they portray violence purely for the sake of violence? That latter point of view is held up for inspection and then dismissed in all its absurdity in the chapter entitled The Violence of Bruce Lee. The Boxing of Muhammad Ali is undeniably violent - some might say savage - but to deny the existence of its art is to close one's eyes to reality.

Another very important, but less talked about facet of Bruce Lee's remarkable prowess is discussed in Chapter Three. Here we are brought to realise the full extent of Lee's brilliance in not only conquering previously untrodden paths of kung-fu ability, but then translating them into terms suitable for the cinema. As our authors point out, working at Lee's normal breakneck pace, it's undoubtedly far easier to actually make contact with an opponent than it is to 'pull' the punch or kick and keep it looking realistic for the camera. Details of just how the Master achieved such incredible levels of realism are recounted here in full, and readers will also get a clearer idea of the almost superhuman standards Lee set himself in his search for perfection.

Finally, as regular readers of *Kung-Fu Monthly* magazine will know, luck recently came by in the guise of a collection of press clippings from around the world, and some of the things the various authors said about Lee have to be seen to be believed. If ever anybody needed reminding about the adage - don't believe all you read in the newspapers - then this is it. Sometimes it really looks as if the reporters were writing up a ball game with one hand and commenting on the Master with the other!

These people get paid to research their work properly and there can be no excuse for besmirching the good name of Bruce Lee with their crass lack of knowledge. Perhaps the only good thing to come out of the whole business is the obvious fact that Lee was totally unaffected by the whole thing. And it's perhaps fair to say that, had the writers scratched just a little below the surface of the Master's four major films, they might have discovered a thing or two about their fatuous and empty comment. Lee was a man of thought, deed and action, and such tools can be used in any field of human endeavour - criticism included! Let's hope that one day, these men may be moved by the strength and spirit of *Bruce Lee in Action*.

Practicing solo is fine up to a point. Here, technique, balance and style can all be perfected. However, developing the necessary rhythm to actually hit something require the cooperation of a willing partner. Here, Bruce spars with a punching mitt held by his wife Linda, with son Brandon looking on and even giving his father a few pointers! As with any sport, the participant must stay in peak physical condition, and in the case of the martial arts this, is more true than most.

BRUCE LEE IN ACTION

As well as a strict diet, Bruce Lee underwent a rigorous training regime, involving daily runs, workouts, and punishing exercises, many involving the use of special apparatus which he kept in his Los Angeles home. Here Bruce undergoes a type of exercise familiar to many but one none the less effective - Skipping.

BRUCE LEE IN ACTION

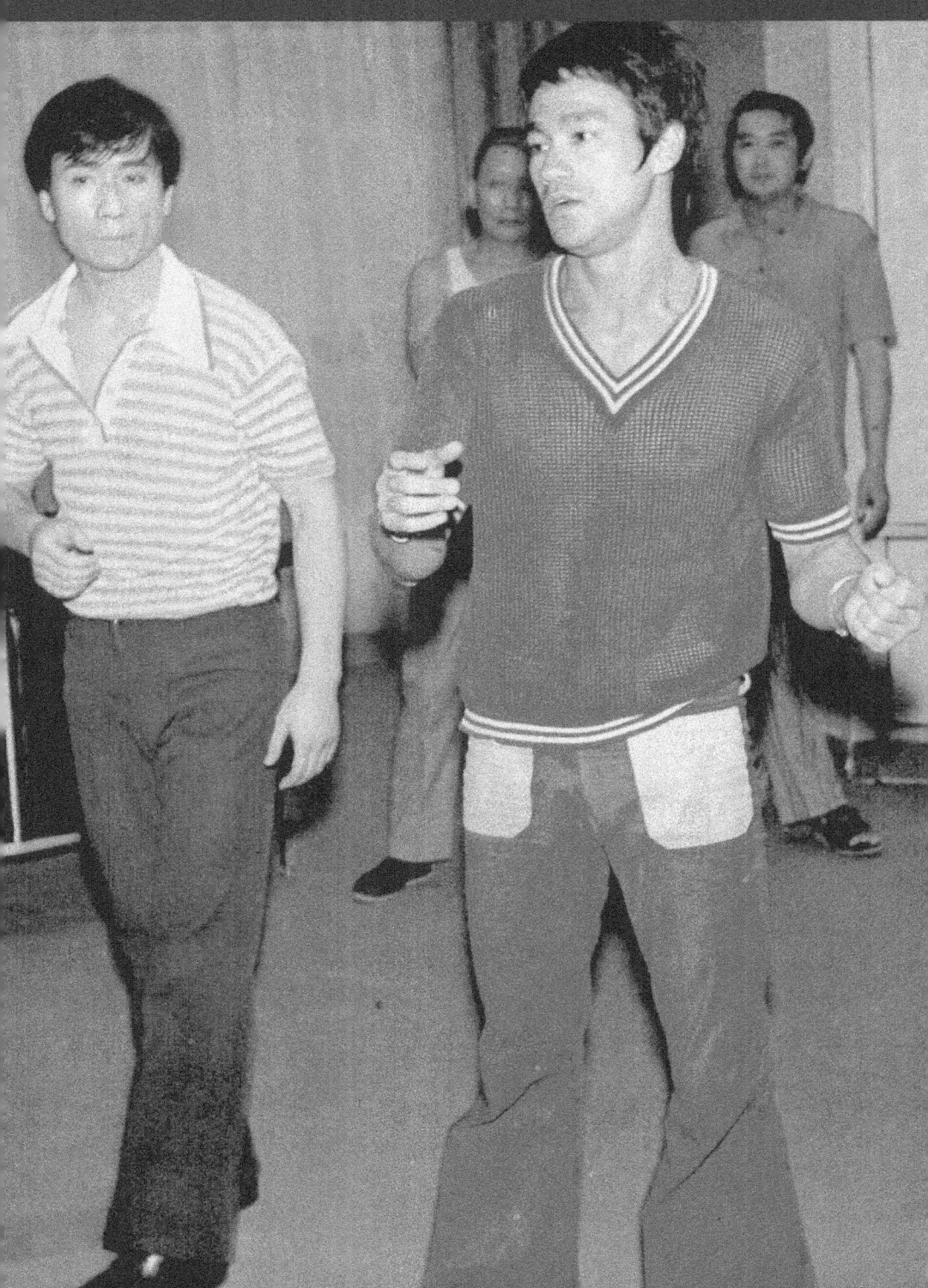

THE KUNG-FU MONTHLY ARCHIVE SERIES

BRUCE LEE IN ACTION

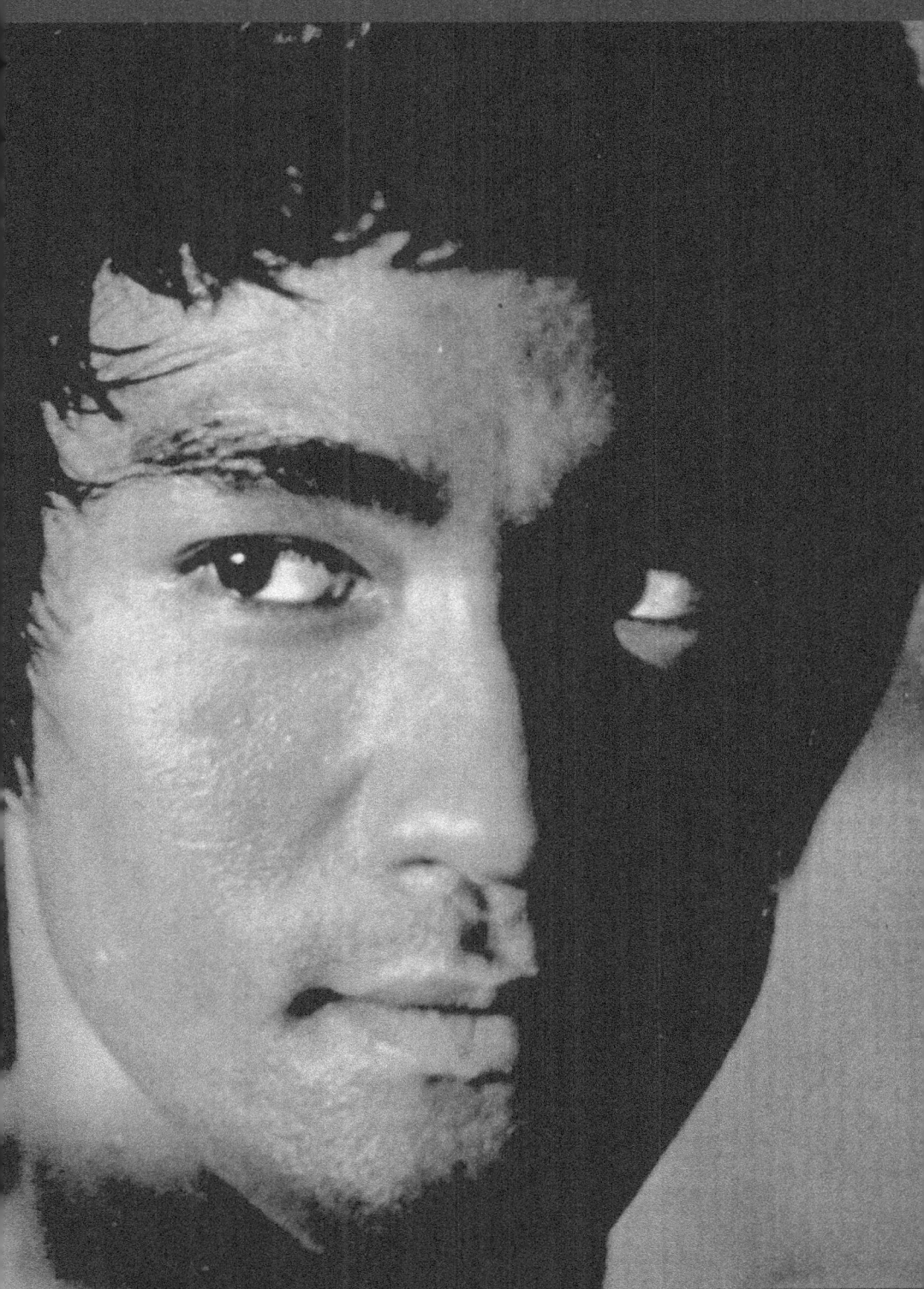

THE KUNG-FU MONTHLY ARCHIVE SERIES

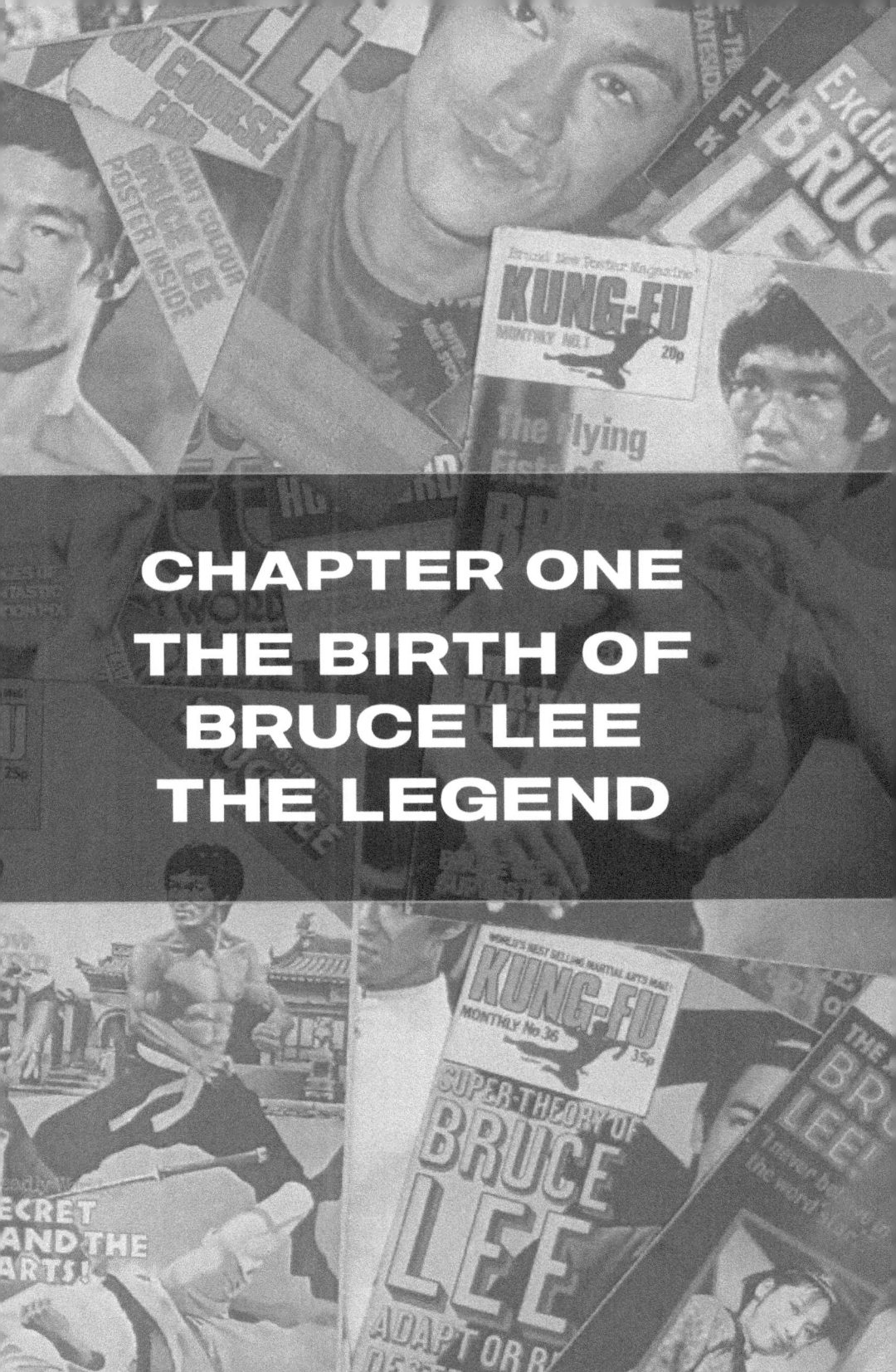

CHAPTER ONE
THE BIRTH OF BRUCE LEE THE LEGEND

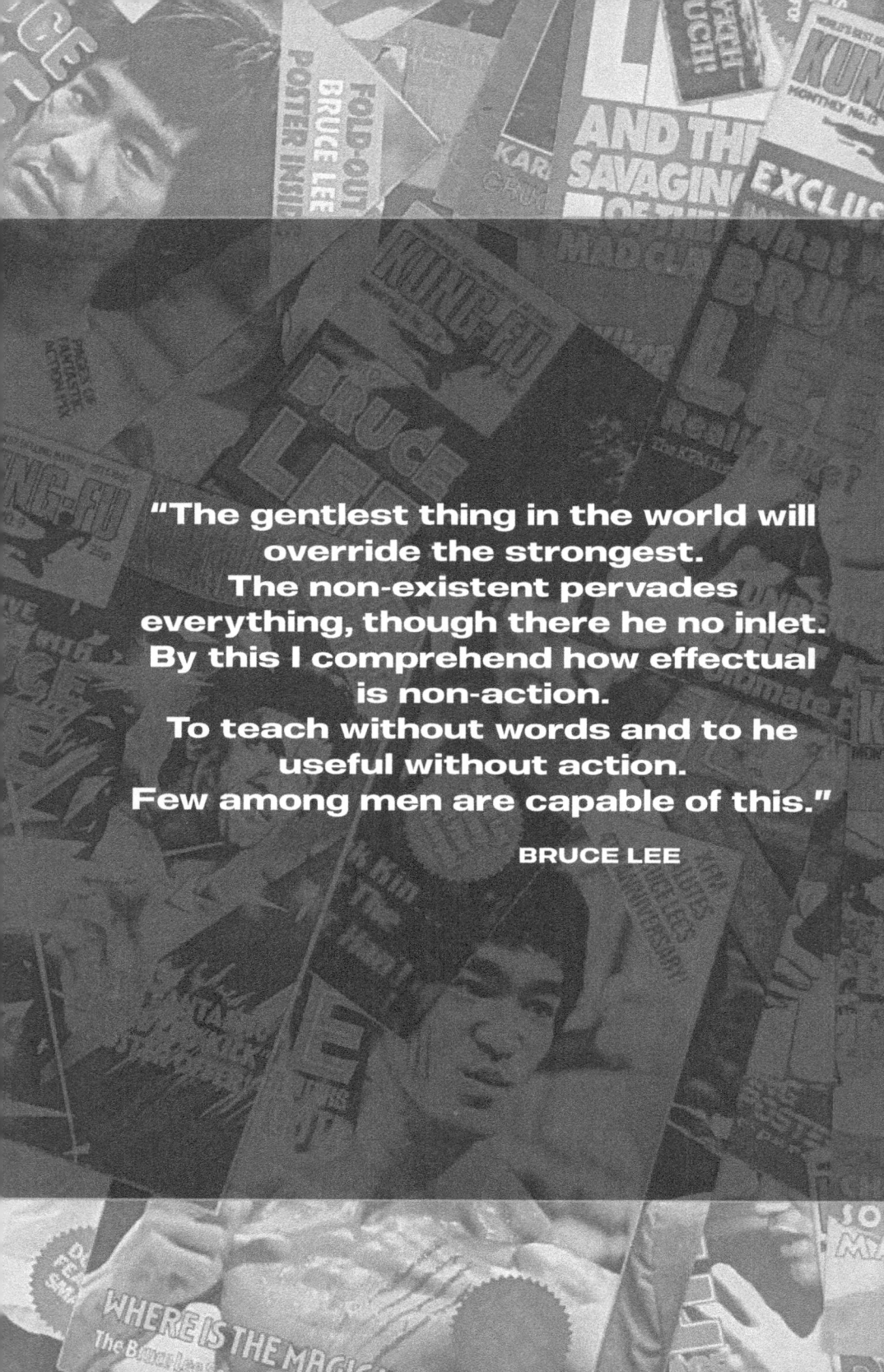

> "The gentlest thing in the world will override the strongest.
> The non-existent pervades everything, though there he no inlet.
> By this I comprehend how effectual is non-action.
> To teach without words and to he useful without action.
> Few among men are capable of this."
>
> **BRUCE LEE**

As the last ferry of the night ploughed through the warm waters of Hong Kong's massive Victoria Harbour, away from the gay night lights of North Point and back towards Kowloon, the small neatly groomed teenager leaning on the forecastle rail was distracted from his memories of the night's party over the water by a raucous laugh.

Slowly, he turned round. The ferry was almost empty. A moment or two ago he had been alone on that particular part of the deck. Now he had company. Two older youths, dressed in the torn and tarnished jeans and vest of the Hong Kong street kids, were standing a yard or two away. Cynically, they looked him up and down from his polished shoes and fitted suit, to his scrubbed face and brylcreemed hair. The teenager knew what was coming.

"Hey," one of them broke the silence. "Are you a boy or a girl?"

The other guffawed. "Looks like a girl to me. Sure dresses nice, don't she? Wanna dance, sis..?"

As the insults grew more and more biting, the teenager turned slowly away from his taunters, leaned back on the rail, and began to think. On the ferry he was safe; the two thugs had nowhere to run away from the law. His problems would only begin in earnest when they docked. The teenager pursed his lips, ignored the barrage of abuse, and continued to think.

The gang-plank crashed onto Kowloon dockside and the teenager turned and made his way towards it, carefully ignoring the two youths following him four or five paces behind, aping his walk and sniggering. He began to take his usual route home, down a quiet backstreet. Hardly believing their luck, his would-be assailants followed. Then, about fifty yards down the street, it happened.

The gentle-faced teenager wheeled quickly round, crouched before the two youths, opened his mouth, and at ear-splitting volume, began to screech every obscenity that came into his mind. Set back by the unexpected sight of this swearing, screaming quarry, it took the larger of the two a moment to compose himself and lumber unsurely towards him. The second troublemaker, disconcerted, remained some yards away. He turned out to be the wiser. As the larger youth approached his raucous victim, the boy stopped shouting, fell to the ground, and WHACK! A shiny patent leather shoe crashed into his attacker's shinbone, sending him reeling headlong onto the pavement, where he lay, clutching his leg and moaning.

His friend's confusion grew, but any ideas he might have entertained about lending a hand were quickly dispelled as the teenager leapt to his feet, recommenced screeching, and hurled himself in the direction of the second youth's waist. Just in time, the thug turned and ran. The teenager stopped, grinned happily, brushed himself down, and continued his walk home with a jaunty step.

From encounters such as this, the young Bruce Lee learnt much about the martial arts. Primarily, of course, he learnt the necessity of having some fighting skill in the concrete jungle of Kowloon. But there were other lessons. The importance of unpredictability in order to distract an opponent, and what he later described as "... complete determination. The worst opponent you can come across is one whose aim has become an obsession. For instance, if a man has decided that he is going to bite off your nose no matter what happens to him in the process, the chances are that he will succeed in doing it. He may be severely beaten up but that will not stop him carrying out his original objective. That

is the real fighter."

    Bruce Lee was always small for his age, a fact that may have contributed more than is generally recognised to his becoming the most skilful proponent of the fighting arts in modern times. In more than one interview, he confirmed that his modest stature led to him bearing the brunt of some serious bullying in his childhood. It was after one particularly vicious attack that Lee decided he needed to seek tuition in self-defence.

    At school, he began sitting behind his desk with one arm pressed hard against the immoveable edge of the wood, hour after hour after hour, until his biceps and forearm muscles stood out like whorls of oak. He persuaded a friendly older student to stay behind after school and spar with him until, within a few months, he was able to track down his previous tormentors and mercilessly extract a painful revenge. It was then that the Bruce Lee legend began to grow. The punk gangs that had once followed him, jeering down the gangplank of the Kowloon ferry, now adopted him as leader. It was a vicious, dog-eat-dog world, and for a while Lee revelled in it, even when the prize for the loser was serious inju-

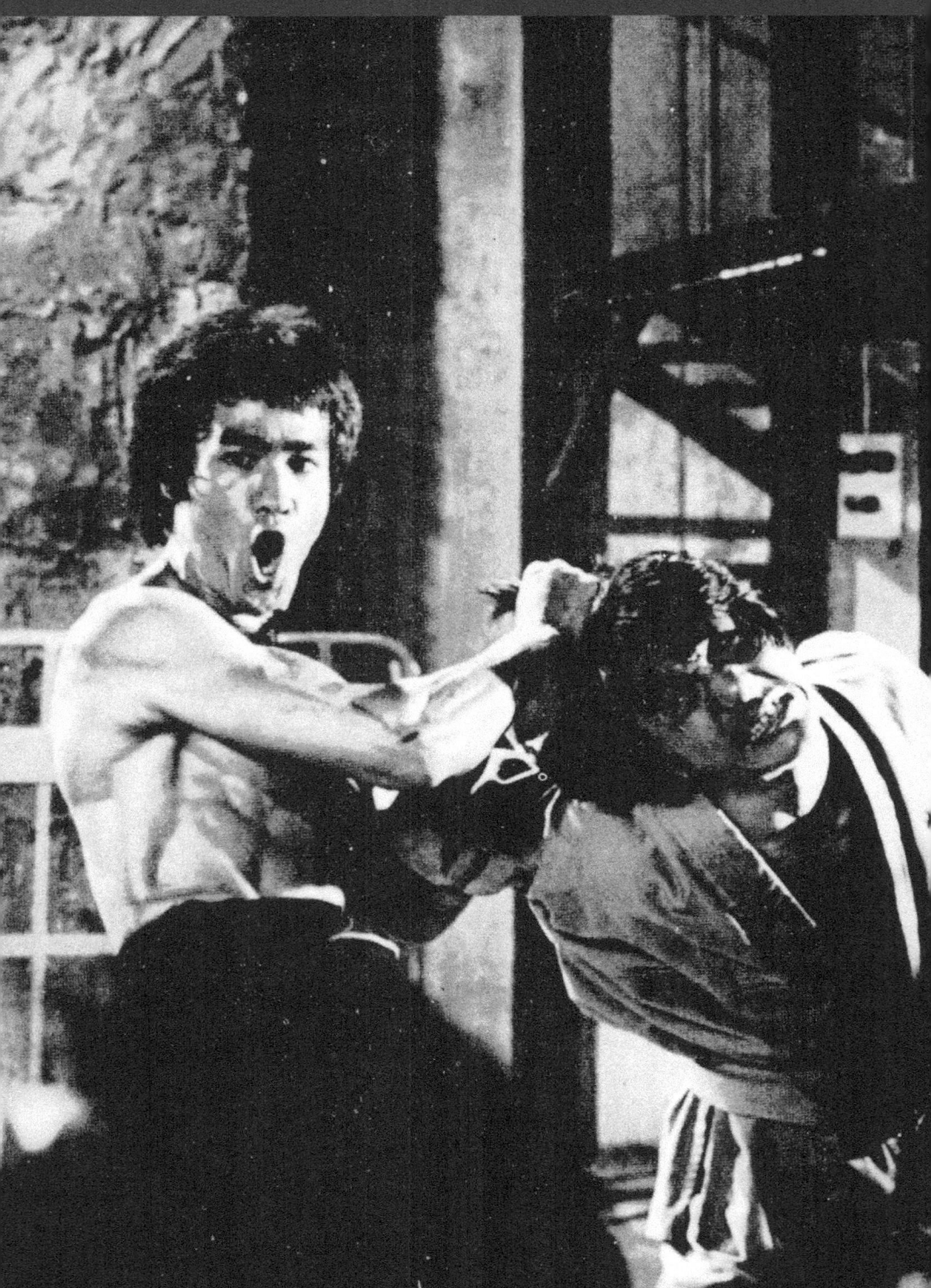

ry or death - as it sometimes had to be. Lee recalled in adulthood this story from his youth.

He had only recently been accepted as leader of his gang, and the leader of a rival gang decided immediately to test his mettle. A fight was arranged on the top of a five-storey apartment block, with the winner being granted the automatic privilege of throwing the loser down onto the street. They reached the top, and Lee turned to speak to a friend. Without warning, his opponent leapt on him, kicking and biting. Infuriated by this lack of courtesy, Lee stormed into action, breaking both his opponent's arms and fracturing his femur in a matter of minutes. He did not, however, toss the unconscious youth over the edge, but called for an ambulance and hurriedly left. In the streets of Hong Kong, the Bruce Lee legend gathered weight.

In his late teens, however, Lee came to understand that street rough-houses and roof-top brawls had their limitations. "As a kid in Hong Kong," he later mused, "I was a punk and went looking for fights. We used chains and pens with knives hidden inside. Then, one day,

THE KUNG-FU MONTHLY ARCHIVE SERIES

BRUCE LEE IN ACTION

On panoramic Malibu beach, Bruce Lee gives a virtuoso demonstration of lightening defense and counter attack against a karate Black Belt.

Both combatants assume variations of the agile cat stance. The body weight is held mainly on the rear foot, leaving the front foot, bent slightly at the knee, ready for forwards and backwards movement or counter attacks with the foot. Lee's opponent holds his right arm forwards at 45° with the knife-hand, while the left hand is held back, palm downwards ready for palm-heel block to cover body and groin.

Lee himself demonstrates a more advanced stance, feet still in the cat position, but forward arm ready to trap his assailant's arm with the tiger claw. His rear hand is in the traditional Shaolin snake position for whipping strikes and slashes to an unprotected face or neck.

Moving round his opponent from this position, Lee delivers a stunning side kick to his opponent's face.

In the photograph above, both men are again in positions preliminary to combat, Lee this time in the Kung Fu horse stance, both hands in the tiger claw form. From here, Bruce counters his attacker's middle line thrust with a block and hooking trap, pulling his man forward off balance to floor him with simultaneous inverted fist and elbow strikes.

As the black belt moves in with a roundhouse or circular blow, Bruce Lee counters immediately with a simultaneous attack - in this case a side thrust-kick to the exposed torso. The knee is drawn up to the abdomen, and the kick is executed by stamping the leg straight out to the side, using the edge of the foot.

BRUCE LEE IN ACTION

As a surprise move, Lee's notorious flying kick can be used to bypass all preliminaries and end the fight at a stroke. Vital to the success of such a manoeuvre is great speed, which of course Lee possessed. Leaping high into the air towards the opponent, the right leg is thrust straight out in a side kick at the top of the jump, attacking the head and neck, possessed of tremendous power and force due to the body weight and momentum.

I wondered what would happen if I didn't have my gang behind me when I got into a fight. I decided to learn how to protect myself and I began to study Kung Fu."

Lee was not the only Hong Kong street kid of the time to take up the ancient martial arts for reasons that were less than spiritual. Many enlisted at such estimable establishments as the Wing Chun School, where Lee found himself under the guidance of one of the oldest and most respected masters, Ip Man. The ancient sage captivated the young gang-leader's interest, and thus were sown the seeds of an unholy marriage between Lee's no-nonsense style of street-fighting and the venerable disciplines of Ip Man's Wing Chun school of the martial arts.

As Lee's friends dropped away, one by one, from the school, their romantic interest in the fighting arts abated by the necessary hours of concentration and practice, Lee determined to stay. It seems quite obvious that from an early age he had no intention of preserving and slavishly adhering to the status quo in the martial arts. His lively imagination and street-fighting background led him to grow as impatient as anybody with the time-honoured, inflexible doctrines of Kung Fu. But Lee realised two things. One, that he needed to amass as much varied knowledge of specialist fighting arts as possible before,

two, he would be considered qualified to have any say in the development of new forms of Kung Fu.

Nonetheless, Bruce Lee in his teens was as volatile a character as Bruce Lee, international film star, and occasionally his impatience would break the surface. "Goddamn it!" he once cried as a teacher suggested some tedious and apparently meaningless exercise, "We have to do that crap again?" To another master foolish enough to ask the aggressive youngster his opinions on Yin and Yang, Lee replied succinctly: "Baloney."

Behind the adolescent rebelliousness, however, lay a sincere conviction learnt on the streets of Kowloon that fighting was about beating an opponent in physical combat. That all of the katas, all of the schools - both hard and soft - that the concept of *Tao* and the learned teachings of Lao Tzu, Bodidharma and Ip Man, were utterly pointless unless geared to that end. Philosophical concepts in the martial arts were not goals in themselves, but means by which one could perfect ability as a fighter. "Too much horsing around with unrealistic stances and classical forms and rituals," wrote Lee some years later. "It's just too artificial and mechanical and doesn't really prepare a student for actual combat. A guy could get clobbered while getting into his classical mess. Classical methods like these, which I consider a form of paralysis, only solidify and condition what was once fluid. Their practitioners are merely blindly rehearsing systematic routines and stunts that will lead to nowhere."

These were strong words indeed to shout down the hallowed corridors of the traditional martial arts world, words to excite controversy and criticism. And Lee knew that all of his finely phrased attacks on the old school would be derided, laughed out of court, unless he could replace the outmoded styles with a new, contemporary, and above all, effective approach of his own. Hence the development and consequent announcement from his gymnasium in Seattle, of Jeet Kune Do.

The early days of Jeet Kune Do, predictably, were not without controversy and inci-

dent. Even though Lee had escaped Hong Kong to seek an education and a new life in the USA, there were sufficient practitioners of the martial arts on that side of the Pacific to take offence at the young upstart's impertinence in questioning the validity of the old forms. He even declared them all a hidebound waste of time and started a new school. Twice Lee was approached by two martial artists wanting to settle the score. A master from San Francisco's Chinatown called Wong Jack Man was pressed into service by several of his friends and followers, and arrived on Lee's doorstep with a challenge carefully inscribed on a scroll. Lee was expected to refuse. He was, after all, the younger, less experienced man. But to withdraw from such a challenge would have discredited him, and, more importantly, his revolutionary beliefs. Besides, the streets of Kowloon had taught him that a challenge to fight cannot lightly be set aside.

"No hitting in the face. No kicking in the groin," suggested Wong Jack Man.

Lee turned angrily on him. "I'm not standing for any of that. You've come here with an ultimatum and a challenge, hoping to scare me off. You've made the challenge, so I'm making the rules, and it's no-holds-barred. All-out". Fortunately for the brash young exponent of Jeet Kune Do, it took him no more than a few minutes to outclass Wong Jack

Man and, with the older fighter's followers begging for the contest to be stopped, extract a submission.

At a demonstration in Seattle, Lee found himself the object of taunts by a Japanese karate black belt, who constantly interrupted Lee's lecture on Jeet Kune Do with invitations to a fight "next week." Finally Lee, exasperated, replied "Why not now?" and within seconds yet another opponent was left wishing that he'd seen rather less of the art of Jeet Kune Do.

The most insidious, and - to Lee's point of view - harmful taunts were yet to be cast, however, and they proved too intangible for the Little Dragon, (as he came to be known) to crush by speed of foot and fist. Gradually, word spread that Jeet Kune Do was really nothing more than a distortion of the Wing Chun style that Lee had learned in Hong Kong from Ip Man - a distortion, it was rumoured, that was only feasible because of Lee's two physical defects: his shortness, and the fact that one of his legs was said to be slightly longer than the other. These astonishing slanders gained ground, and sapped Lee's once unassailable credibility throughout the last few years of his life. They also probably placed an almost unbearable strain on his once-affectionate relationship with his old tutor.

Certainly, Ip Man appeared responsible either consciously or unconsciously, for originating certain of these wounding assertions. He told Sifu Leung Ting, (who proceeded to tell anybody who cared to listen), that, "Because of his physical defect, Bruce cannot squat on his heels, but he is a diligent child, and one day he quietly said to me: 'Guess whether I can squat on my heels.' 'Of course not.' I replied. Bruce whispered mysteriously, 'You want to bet?' From these words, I knew that he had conquered his physical defect by his industrious spirit."

Crediting Bruce Lee with an industrious spirit did not fully compensate for taking away his reputation as an original however, and Lee may possibly have harboured something of a grudge against Ip Man. A grudge which, it's said, led to an incident which shocked and horrified Hong Kong. In 1973, the old Sifu died, and from all over the world, practitioners of Wing Chun - old friends, admirers, and representatives of most styles of Chinese martial arts - attended the funeral rites. Lee, who was in Hong Kong filming at the time, missed the ceremony. Newspaper editorials railed against him, the public took great offence, and popular response to the incident was perfectly depicted in a cartoon that appeared in one of Hong Kong's magazines. It showed Lee tugging his forelock at the shrine of Ip Man and saying "Sorry, Master, I am too busy making money to go to your funeral ceremony."

For whatever reason he failed to attend, the reputation of Bruce Lee was reportedly dented in a way that, a year or two earlier, would hardly have seemed possible. Any struggle to vindicate himself and his fighting art would be a hard and bitter one.

In many ways, such struggles continue to this day. In his defence, two points might well be worth considering. Firstly, Lee's single-handed attempt to rationalise and reform Kung Fu understandably made him many enemies. One could hardly hope to make monster omelettes without breaking a few eggs on the way. Secondly, Lee was extraordinarily talented, wealthy and famous. Wealth, talent and fame inevitably draw jealousy and criticism like iron filings to a magnet. Had Lee not died so early, he might well have succeeded in defusing any backlash without compromising his fundamental position - for Lee was a man who barely understood the meaning of compromise. In the event, he died a man with few friends, and many enemies.

BRUCE LEE IN ACTION

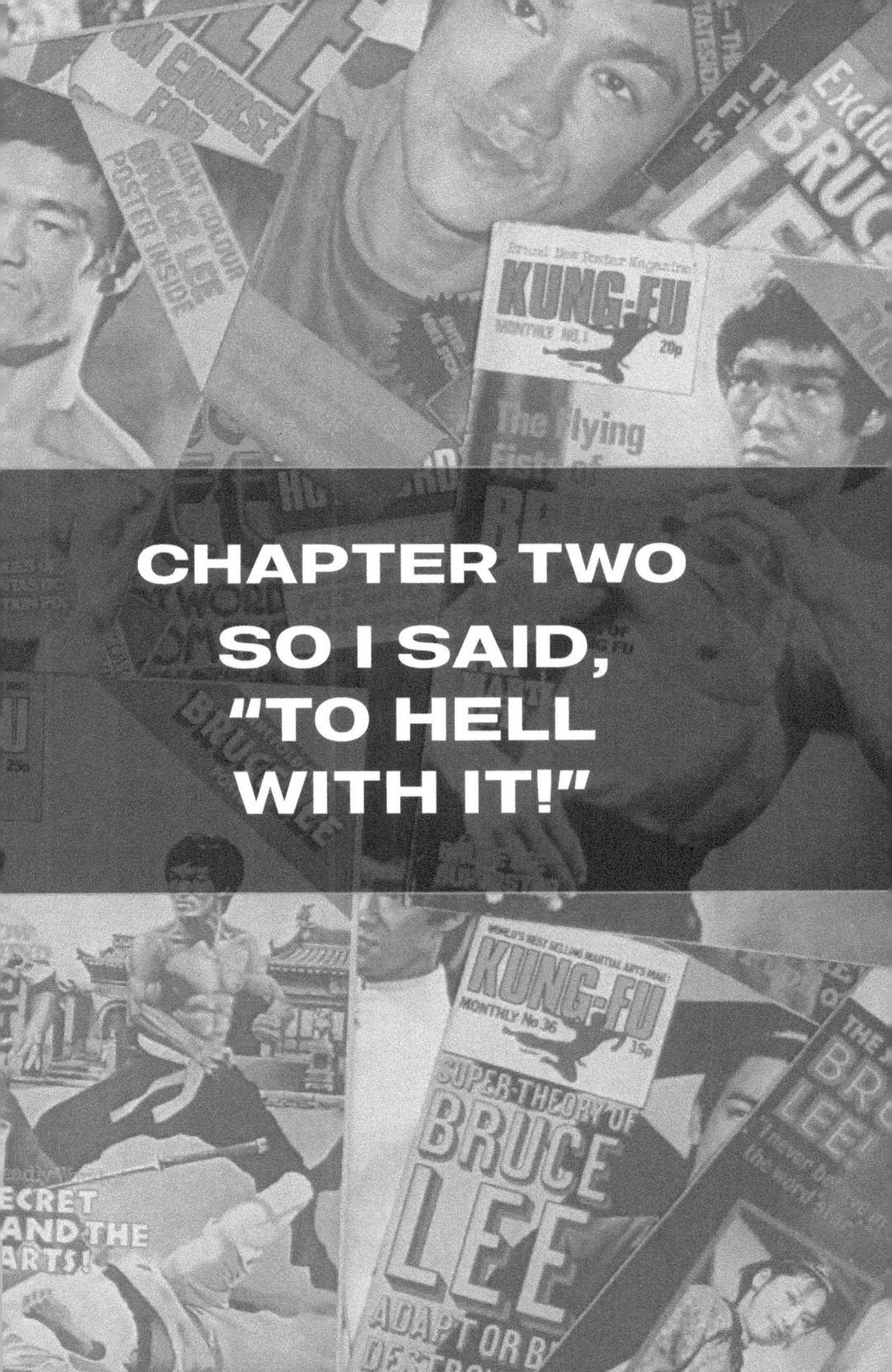

CHAPTER TWO
SO I SAID, "TO HELL WITH IT!"

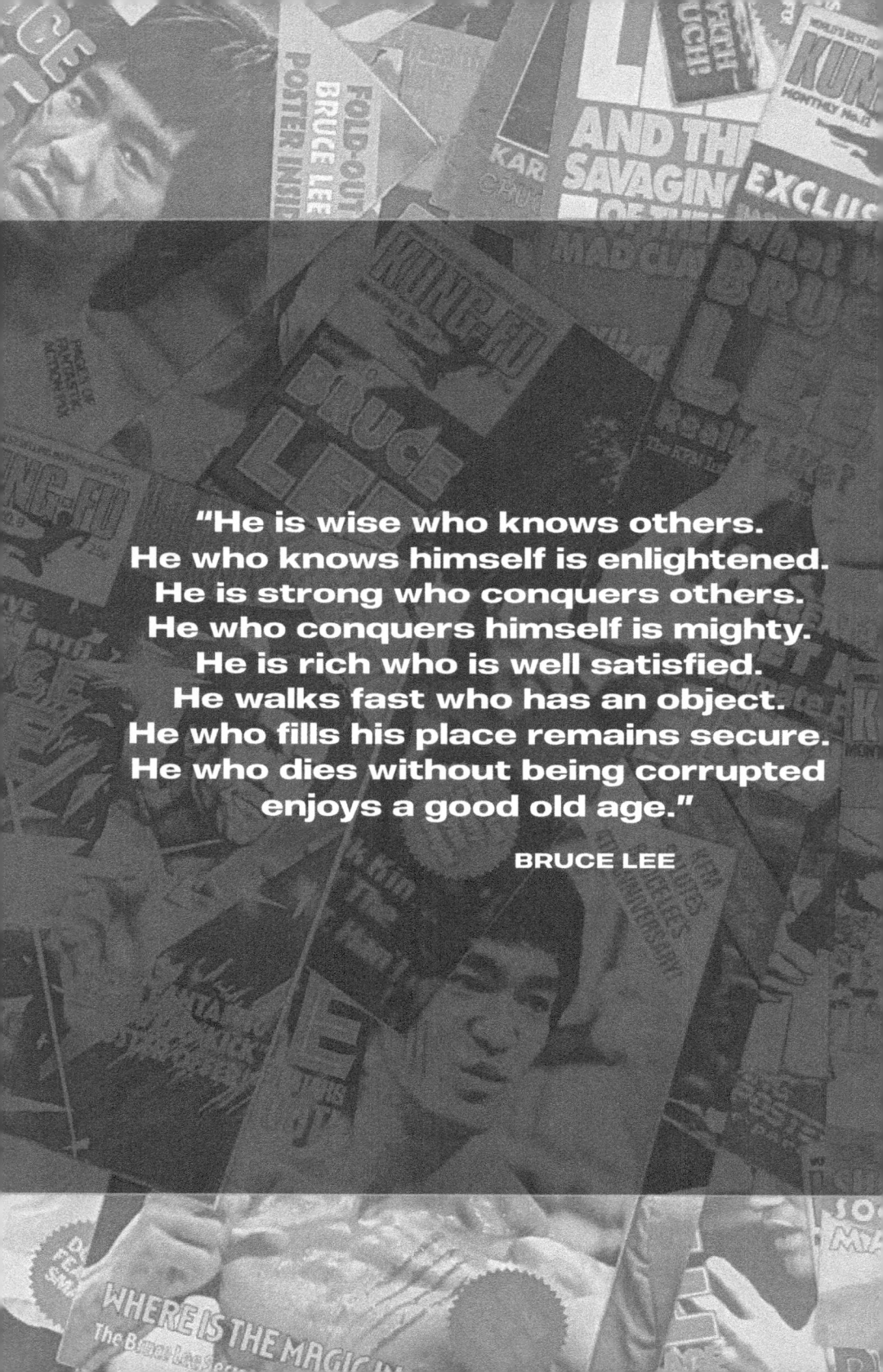

"He is wise who knows others.
He who knows himself is enlightened.
He is strong who conquers others.
He who conquers himself is mighty.
He is rich who is well satisfied.
He walks fast who has an object.
He who fills his place remains secure.
He who dies without being corrupted
enjoys a good old age."

BRUCE LEE

BRUCE LEE IN ACTION

If the world will not come to Jeet Kune Do, take Jeet Kune Do to the world. As Bruce Lee hurled himself into the maelstrom of the movie business, that could well have been his motto. Anxiously aware of how much he had to prove, Lee's involvement with his movies was never less than complete: a total mix of his razor-sharp mind and fantastically tuned body.

His first major film, *The Big Boss*, could hardly have been bettered as a vehicle for Lee's unique talents. He left America with what appeared at the time to be vain and empty boasts of becoming the biggest movie star in the world. He wanted to go back to Hong Kong to use the native movie industry there in much the same way that Clint Eastwood had used the Italian "spaghetti western" industry to thumb a ride to fame. Many people assumed that Lee would never be back or if he did return, it would be a crestfallen, humbler man than the cocky upstart who had left to attempt the impossible.

History, of course, tells a different story. In *The Big Boss*, Lee's fighting ability is kept under wraps for the first half of the film. He is goaded time and again, almost to breaking point, and restrains himself only by reaching for the locket around his neck, the locket given to him by his mother after she had extracted the promise that he would keep out of trouble and stay away from fights. The brooding power of Lee, stalking the screen like a tiger, exuding all the pregnant threat of an unexploded bomb, kept audiences first in Asia and later throughout the West gripping the arms of their cinema seats until finally the locket chain snaps, and with it Lee's patience.

In the history of cinema, there have never been scenes such as those which greeted the arrival of Bruce Lee, Movie Giant. As the extraordinary battle in *The Big Boss* reached its climax, Lee's powerful fists were pumping faster than the eye could follow, like twin pistons into the slowly collapsing chest of his last opponent. In Asia, audiences leapt to their feet and onto the backs of their chairs, shouting applause and acclamation. Raymond Chow, the man who had considered it necessary to launch a massive publicity campaign just to help the film break even in Asia, realised that he had an international record-breaker on his hands. Throughout Europe and America the word spread, and the Bruce Lee cult became an obsession with millions of cinema-goers.

Behind the scenes, Lee was determined not to compromise his art. The fight scenes that thrilled the world are, as nearly as can be expected of the cinema, real. Of course, Lee does not actually pummel his opponent to death in *The Big Boss*, the punches are pulled (which at that speed is surely a more difficult task than actually landing them), and his victim explodes a "blood sac" concealed in his mouth, to spit out the gore from his supposedly ruptured chest. In the same way, a hatchet in the back is actually buried into a lump of hollowed-out wood, which also contains screen "blood", and is strapped to the recipient's back. A dagger or sword, plunged into an actor's flesh, actually has a retractable blade which, on contact, retreats back into the handle, triggering off a spurt of blood as it goes.

But apart from such scenes which obviously have to be faked, an astoundingly high proportion of Lee's stunts, in fights or otherwise, are filmed as he performed them - the uncanny leaps, the perfect accuracy of the hook kicks, the speed of the feints and punches are all cinema verite. In fact, they are occasionally slowed down so that an audience can actually see what Lee is doing! Of all martial artists, Lee geared his fights above anything else for an audience. The walls of a gymnasium that he had specially constructed in Amer-

THE KUNG-FU MONTHLY ARCHIVE SERIES

ica were lined with mirrors, so that he could study his own actions. For the same reason, he took to filming his workouts on videotape and playing them back later, watching for every slight error, aiming always to make more visible and obvious the care and genius that was behind his every move. That said, it has to be admitted that one particular scene, not involving blood or death, was faked - a fact that should not particularly surprise anybody who has seen it. When, in *Fist of Fury*, Lee lifts Mr Wu above head height while Mr Wu is sitting in a rickshaw, he has the assistance of two helpers, lifting up the rickshaw from outside camera shot. Nor is Mr Wu actually Mr Wu - he's a life-size, light model. Not even that paragon of the martial arts, Bruce Lee, could pull that one off unassisted.

During the making of *Fist of Fury*, it was becoming increasingly obvious to those close to him that despite having been promoted to co-director in only his second film - Bruce Lee was getting frustrated with the Hong Kong film industry. He had never held it in particularly high regard, having talked of the Mandarin movies as, "Awful - everybody fights all the time, and what really bothered me was that they all fought in exactly the same way. When you get into a fight, everybody reacts differently, and it is possible to act and fight at the same time."

It had seemed for a time, however, that the beneficial influence Lee was having, and the rewards that this was reaping for him both materially and in terms of public acclaim, might be enough to persuade him to stay. Sadly, though, it was not to be. In a remarkable interview, he told the *Hong Kong Standard*:

"I'm dissatisfied with the expression of the cinematic art here in Hong Kong. It's time somebody did something about the films here. There are simply not enough soulful characters here who are committed, dedicated, and are at the same time, professionals."

"I didn't create this monster - all this gore in the Mandarin films. It was there before I came. At least I don't spread violence. I don't call the fighting in my films violence. I call it action. An action film borders somewhere between reality and fantasy. If it were completely realistic, you would call me a bloody, violent man. I would simply destroy my opponent by tearing him apart or ripping his guts out. I wouldn't do it so artistically. I have this intensity in me, the audience believes in what I do. But I act in such a way as to border my action somewhere between reality and fantasy."

"I can't express myself fully on film here, or the audiences wouldn't understand what I was talking about half the time. That's why I can't stay in South-East Asia all the time. I am improving and making new discoveries every day. If you don't, you are already crystallised and that's it."

Bruce Lee had handed in his notice to the cinema industry of South-East Asia after using it to make two films which had rocketed him into the history books as the biggest star of all time. He had another world to conquer.

And so it was that Lee returned, in triumph, to Hollywood. This was not his first foray into the fairyland of moving pictures. The first time had had its small successes, bit parts in TV serials such as *Longstreet*, a small but violent scene - smashing up James Garner's office with impeccable style -in the film *Marlowe*, but by and large, Hollywood had not exactly taken Bruce Lee into its bosom in those earlier days. Lee explains:

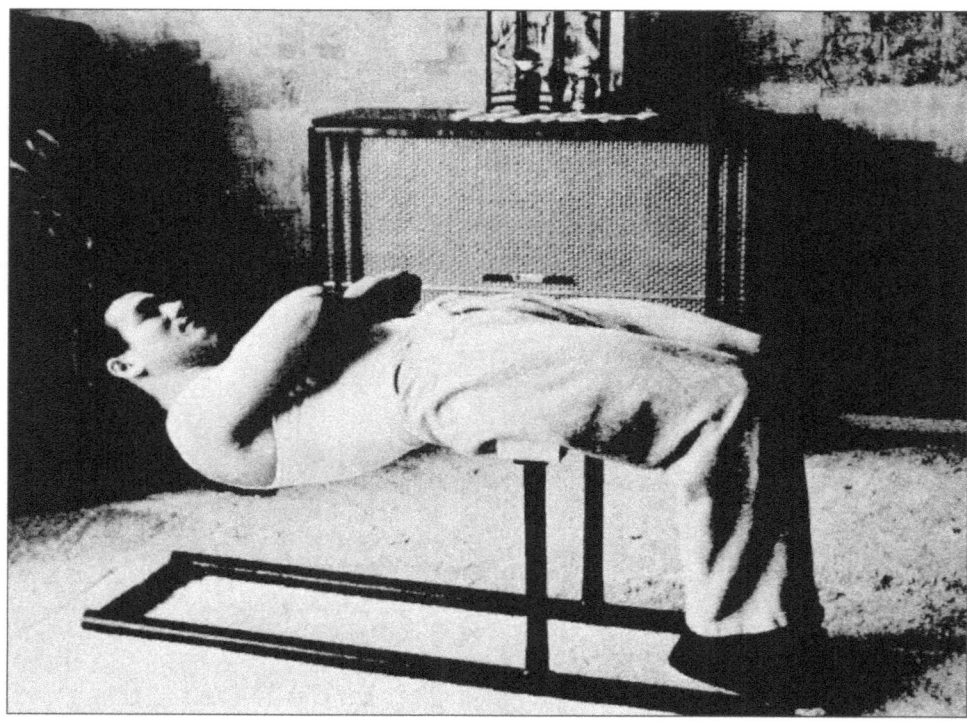

BRUCE LEE IN ACTION

Here, in characteristically superb form, Bruce Lee illustrates one of the most difficult classical exercises of Kung Fu; the line form, or kata.

Although Lee himself scorned too rigid an adherence to such forms, which represent a series of moves performed against an imaginary opponent, especially in actual combat, he recognised them as a means towards an end in developing muscular tension, balance, and an all important flow of movement in combination attack and defence.

In the first picture, he assumes the ready position, feet together, body upright, and the arms held forward, bent at 45° with the fists held face upwards. Taking a short breath, the abdomen is tensed and a double spear-hand thrust performed to opponent's solar plexus.

Transferring the body weight onto the left foot, both hands are brought upwards and outwards, performing a double roundhouse block with the wrists, covering the head and body, while Lee assumes the cat stance. In this stance, 70% of the body weight rests on the rear foot, the front foot resting lightly on the ground ready for an instantaneous kick. Both knees are held slightly bent. Moving into the horse stance, Bruce Lee executes a double side thrust with the first two knuckles of each fist. The left foot is the drawn back slightly into a variation of the cat stance, facing to the left. The left arm blocks downwards in the low line, while the right hand is held back over the head in the tiger claw position, ready for either blocking or striking as necessary.

Finally, Bruce moves in to finish off his opponent with his devastating and unstopable punch, stepping forward on the right foot to add his momentum and weight into the punch. Note the left fist simultaneously drawn back to the belt to add counter-force to the blow.

"Here I am, a Chinese, not prejudiced or anything, just realistic. How many times in Hollywood films is a Chinese required? And when it is required, it is always branded as the typical 'tung-dung-tung-tung-tung,' with the little pigtail at the back - you know the type. So I said, 'The hell with it.'"

Stirling Silliphant, a Hollywood scriptwriter who had faith in Lee from the earliest days, continues the story. "Some of the struggles Bruce had while getting really heavily involved in films read like a scene out of any really grim fight against prejudice. Bruce would never play the chop-chop pigtail coolie. Everyone admired him for that. He insisted on being human."

Indeed, but it could be argued back that when Lee took his refusal to be a kow-towing Chinaman to its logical conclusion, when in that glorious moment in *Fist of Fury*, he soared into the air to tear down and shatter the sign outside the Japanese-run public park which read "NO DOGS OR CHINAMEN" - then Lee became more than human. And Hollywood was always interested in immortals.

So Lee returned to the dream factory, in the enviable position of being able to select his studio. He chose Warner Bros, mainly, he claimed, because of a great respect for Ted Ashley, Warners' Chairman, to whom he wrote:

"Nowadays, my offers for doing a film have reached a point which I guarantee will both surprise as well as shock you. Viewing from the angle of efficient practical business sense, I hope we will be fair and square and have mutual trust and confidence - I have had a bad experience doing a picture with some person or organisation in Hong Kong. In other words, I was burned once - and didn't like it."

Some friends, however, explained Lee's anxiety to join Warners in another way - they remembered how, some years ago, Bruce had considered himself a favourite for the lead part in a big new martial arts TV series about to be launched by Warners, to be called *The Warrior*. Disappointingly for Lee, Warners eventually gave the part to a westerner, David Carradine, and renamed the series *Kung Fu*. Even Lee, then, still had something to prove, some bad memories to exorcise.

It did not take him long to do so. The stars that he found himself rubbing shoulders with, both on and off the Hollywood set, were quick to recognise the extraordinary talent in their midst. Steve McQueen, for one, said later: "The good head that he acquired was through him knowing himself. He and I used to have great long discussions about that. No matter what you do in life, if you don't know yourself, you're never going to be able to appreciate anything. That, I think, is today's mark of a good human being - to know yourself."

McQueen was not the only admirer of the eastern superstar who was in the process of taking the West by storm. James Coburn, George (James Bond) Lazenby, Jim Kelly, Bob Wall, Chuck Norris - all bowed to the bright light of Lee's talent. To watch him filming was, to the eyes of actors bred on stuntmen and trick photography, an illuminating experience. Lee determined, as usual, to play as much of the action for real as possible, and in *Enter the Dragon*, this caused some unnecessary moments of genuine violence. One scene required a fight between Bob Wall - no mean martial artist himself - and Lee, with Wall given the head start of using two broken bottles. Normal Hollywood etiquette would rule that the bottles be made of toffee, or some harmless synthetic substance. Bob Wall recalls: "I grabbed a bottle in each hand, smashed off the bottoms and got set. I looked down at the jagged ends - they were lethal weapons all right. It surprised me even more when I found

out they were real glass. All Bruce said was, 'Come on at me.' It went perfectly, but unfortunately the scene had to be shot again from another angle. This time, however, Bruce moved a fraction of a second too early and his fist crunched straight into the glass. Spurts of blood flew into the camera and over the floor."

Nor was that the end of the minor injuries and risks run by Lee - he had to receive medical treatment after mixing it with a cobra which had previously, and most fortunately, had most of its poison taken out. He did get his own back, it must be said. He nearly drowned another actor by pushing him out of a boat with just too much force! There were risks implicit in playing opposite Bruce Lee!

If Lee's personal satisfaction at gaining Hollywood's acceptance for an oriental actor was immense, however, even greater still was his delight at the world's acclaim for his fighting skills - his "style that is no style and is all styles" - Jeet Kune Do. What his fellow actors, directors, cameramen, and ultimately audiences were marvelling at, although few of them knew it, was the perfection of a fighting system that was as beautiful to watch as it was impossible to beat, that was graceful and deadly, theatrical and effective. It was not a technique hamstrung by tradition, or obsessed by certain standard moves. If necessary,

BRUCE LEE IN ACTION

In the first sequence of these rare photographs of Bruce Lee and black belt Danny Inosanto, Bruce Lee demonstrates a series of basic defence and counter attack measures.

In the first photograph, Lee parries a right handed attack by his opponent, and traps the attacking arm, pulling forward simultaneously to throw his opponent off balance while delivering a retaliatory knife hand strike to the throat.

As his opponent attacks with a right handed thrust, Lee blocks and traps with his right hand, pulling his assailant off balance once again.

Simultaneous counter attack is executed with a short sharp knuckle strike to the head or body. Bruce Lee in the example follows this immediately with a backhand inverted fist strike to subdue his opponent.

THE KUNG-FU MONTHLY ARCHIVE SERIES

Lee would bite an opponent, or scratch him, or punch him directly on the nose, if no other move was open to him. He believed in the martial arts of simplicity. He even went so far as to deny that Jeet Kune Do was any style at all, telling *Black Belt* magazine: "Let it be understood once and for all that I have not invented a new style, composite, or modification. I have in no way set Jeet Kune Do within a distinct form governed by laws that distinguish it from 'this' style or 'that' method. On the contrary; I hope to free my comrades from bondage to styles, patterns, and doctrines."

One of the better ways of appreciating Lee's philosophy is to watch him fighting more than one person at the same time. In such situations, there simply is not time or room to limit one's fighting arsenal according to the dictates of a certain style. As one opponent is smashed brutally in the face, another is approaching from behind, he must be caught with a windmill kick - and then a third must be dodged, to gain time, before dismissing him with a kick to the groin. No time or effort should be wasted; the beauty of the action lies in its perfect economy. "The height of cultivation," said Lee, "is nothing special. It is merely simplicity, the ability to express the utmost with the minimum. It is the halfway cultivation that leads to ornamentation."

Enter the Dragon was intended to be a cheap production (by Hollywood standards), but by the time the perfectionism of Lee had demanded retake after retake, it ran over budget, and ended up costing more than a million dollars. The accountants need not have worried, though. *Enter the Dragon* repaid its original investment in no time at all and Lee, at last, was firmly established as a western star.

Not all of the horizon was clear, though. Lee found his films encountering a problem that he had hardly considered, a problem that could - if it grew any more difficult - cut the legs away from under his phenomenal western success. Bruce Lee found his films being cut by the censors.

It was a problem that he had hardly considered because in Asia, violence with its accompanying blood and gore is an accepted part of the cinema. It is regarded as a necessary part of movies about the martial arts. When Chinese films first began arriving in the West, they were of limited appeal and consequently mainly shown in cinema clubs, unaffected by film censorship. But when Bruce Lee turned eastern films into mass-audience successes, and they came to be accepted by the biggest distribution companies, the censors made their entrance.

At first, they could not see the beauty and balletic perfection of Lee's action sequences for the blood and guts that are an intrinsic part of fight scenes, and hatchet attacks were cut from *The Big Boss*, along with one or two spurts of blood from the Little Dragon's victims. Lee had anticipated some alteration in the presentation of his Hong Kong films to a western audience; he had after all, always maintained that the gore in the Mandarin movies was too much for the West. But when, for instance, the UK censors got round to taking out the nunchakus scene from *The Way of the Dragon*, and other essential parts of fight scenes were clumsily slashed as well, it became obvious that things were being taken too far. Another disturbing development in the UK was the almost automatic slapping of an 'adults only' certificate on any Bruce Lee (or even any other Kung Fu) film, which in turn prevented some of Lee's greatest fans - the under-eighteen year olds - from seeing their idol. The dubious reason given for this was often that "impressionable" youth would take to imitating the Master, with bloody consequences throughout the city streets of Britain

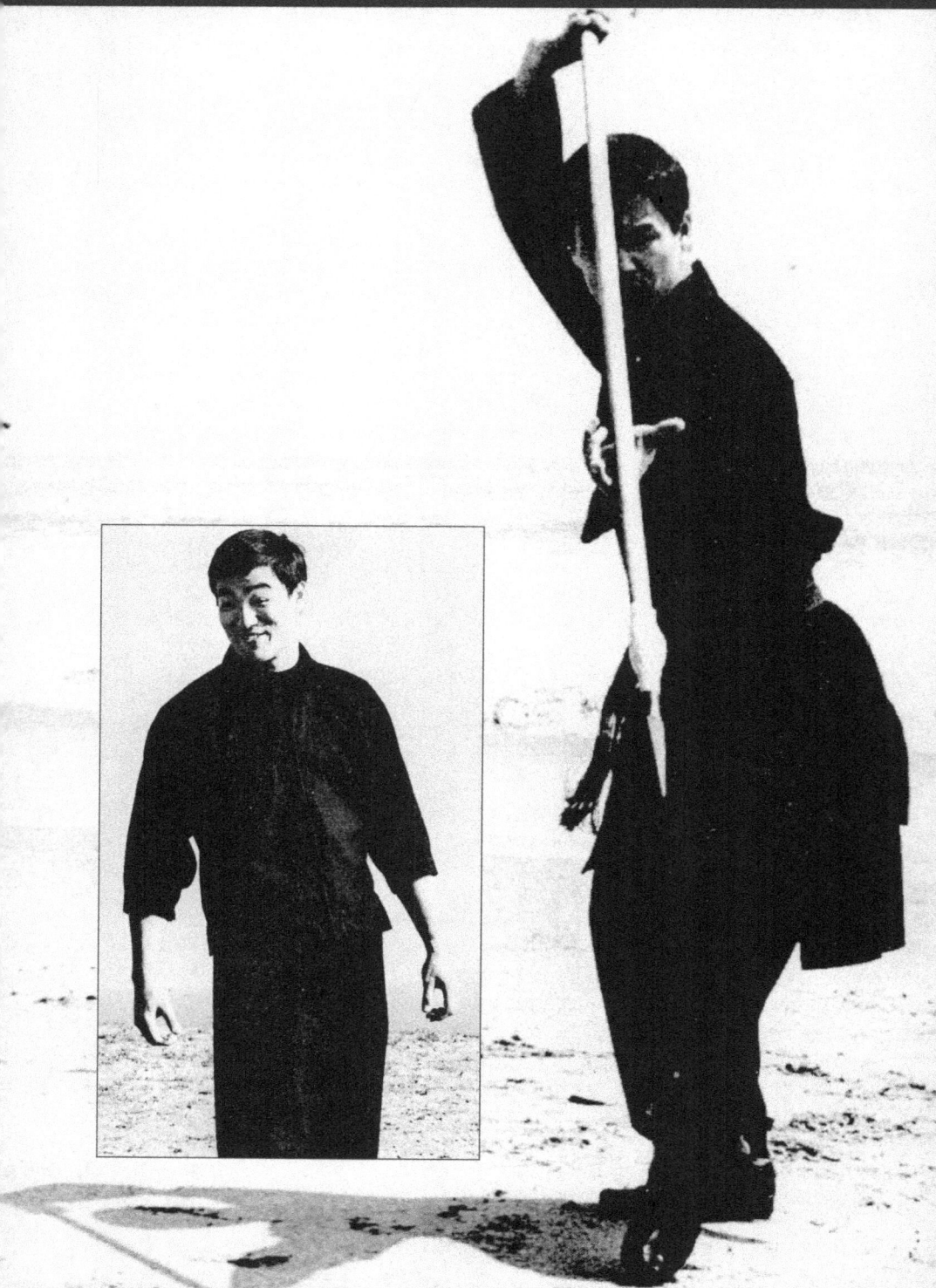

and America. If only imitating Bruce Lee was that easy!

An authority on censorship, interviewed by *Kung Fu Monthly*, had this to say:

"I think the censors have an attitude in general against Chinese pictures. I'll explain why. You could have, say, an American martial arts picture, an Australian martial arts picture, and a Hong Kong martial arts picture. You will find that the American one will come back almost intact, the Australian one will have a few cuts and the Hong Kong film will be butchered! Why? I suppose the way of thinking is that the American companies have put up more money and devoted more time and effort and so they deserve better rewards. I'm not at all convinced that age should be a criteria for judging whether or not fans should be able to see Bruce Lee films. I think the customers are there primarily to appreciate the Little Dragon's enormous skill and personality and I believe the 'adults only' rating to be quite unnecessary."

If any outside body could have helped Lee in his fight against censorship, it must surely have been the press - a body that one would have expected to stand up against the unnecessary limiting of freedom of expression. As it turned out, things were not that simple.

In the sequence of three photographs, taken with a motor drive camera, Bruce Lee illustrates the technique of his notorious flying kick. The first photograph shows the start of the leap, performed on the spot, using both legs to give the necessary spring, arms outstretched to give extra momentum and balance. The knee of the kicking leg is drawn up ready to execute the kick at the apex of the leap. The kicking foot is thrust straight out to the side to produce a devastating blow. Note the concentration on Bruce's face as he performs the most difficult of manoeuvres.

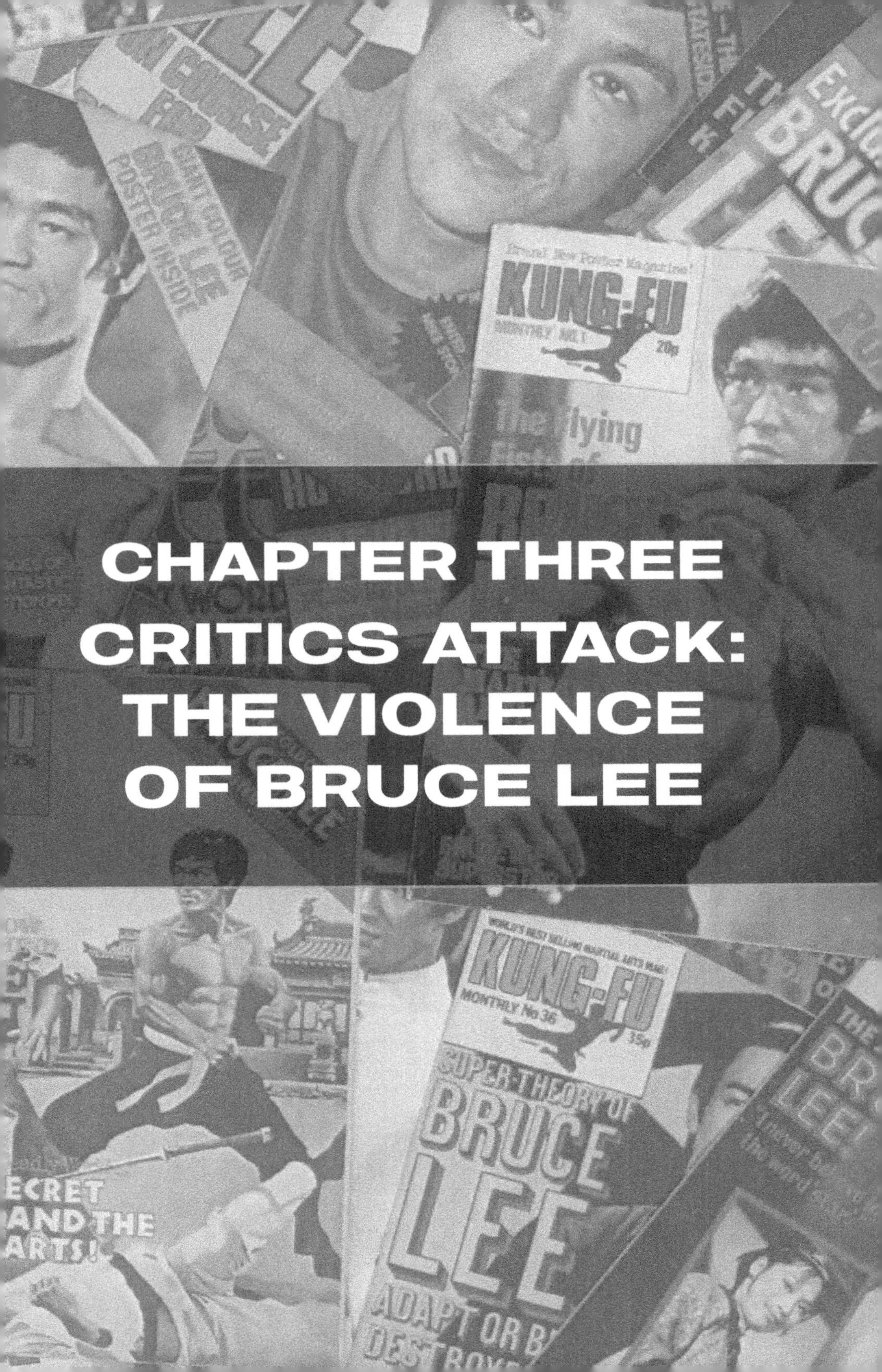

CHAPTER THREE
CRITICS ATTACK: THE VIOLENCE OF BRUCE LEE

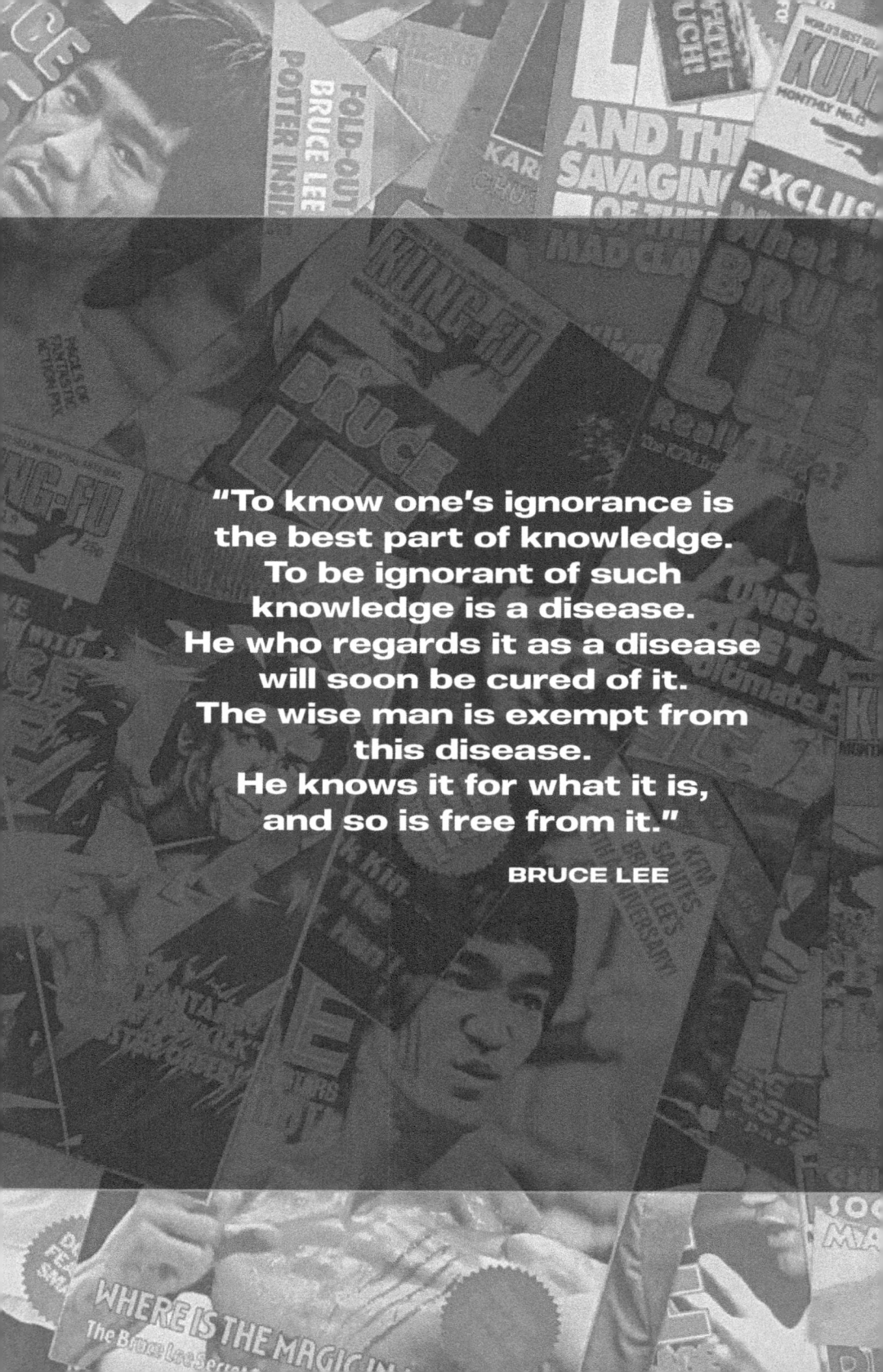

"Frankly I am amazed that audiences have become so hooked on this Oriental garbage."

"The story, the performances, and the production as a whole are laughably naive - just about as sophisticated as beans on toast."

"What is obvious to simple-minded souls such as me about the popularity of such films is their appeal to audiences via the belief that you can have your cake and eat it. Indignation is all right so long as it is righteous. Killing is fine if the slaughter is committed in the name of honour. Death can be excused if the people upon whom it is perpetrated are seen to be as plastic as any puppet in TV's Thunderbirds. Everything is always skin-deep. Black or white. And the blurring of moral distinctions that, paradoxically, it implies is a smudging of values which I find most unpleasant; a witness to the cynical way in which the producers of these movies believe that audiences can be manipulated."

Believe it or not, these are all extracts from reviews of Bruce Lee films, written as the films were released in the West. The critics were not totally unanimous in out-and-out condemnation of Lee's efforts, some were more ferocious than others, but in the early 1970s you would have been hard put to find a critic capable of appreciating and predicting the enormous success that Lee was to enjoy with western audiences.

The three reviews quoted from above are fairly typical of the three varieties of put-down to emanate from the typewriters of critics from Los Angeles to London. The first is of course simply racist - how on earth could decent, respectable cinema-goers, bred on Walt Disney and Doris Day, find anything interesting in a hard, fast, and violent movie from Hong Kong, of all places? The second is a standard, sneering put-down; the type of criticism that has been levelled at great new artists since the beginning of time. The suggestion that naivety and simplicity are somehow "laughable," and to be avoided at all costs by those who wish to make movies, is as absurd as suggesting that the painting of Paul Gauguin is ridiculous because his images have a freshness and innocence that many jaded minds fail to appreciate. Or that, because his syntax is direct and uncomplicated, Ernest Hemingway's writing is "as sophisticated as beans on toast." The third quote, while still misguided, at least makes more of an effort to analyse exactly what it is that the critic finds so obnoxious about Lee's films (this review was headlined: THIS FIST MAKES ME FURIOUS). There, however, rationality stops. Because, surely, despite the writer's heavy-handed attempts at sarcasm ("The lowest form of humour" - Dr Johnson), indignation is all right in a righteous cause. Would the critic suggest that the Chinese were wrong to be indignant at Japanese oppression as depicted in *Fist of Fury*? Of course not. And as for killing being "fine," the message of *Fist of Fury*, as everyone who has seen it knows, couldn't be more opposite. Bruce Lee insists on leaping to an inevitable death before the guns of the Japanese guard in order to atone for the murders he has committed - even though those deaths were carried out in the name of honour. Did James Bond ever show such penitence? Or John Wayne? And is this critic as vituperative in his condemnation of such films as he is of the work of Bruce Lee? Of course not. Bruce Lee was unique in attracting such ferocious criticism in his early days - not only from most of the critics, but also from self-appointed watchdogs of what the public should see and what it shouldn't see. He was a talent so huge that nobody could ignore it, but unfortunately not everybody could understand it. Critics, needing to slot every film into a little pigeonhole, where more furious than most when they found themselves unable to rationalise Lee's genius. His

A short sequence showing Bruce Lee in a lightning series of attack and defence.

Bruce Lee parries a knife attack and while still retaining hold of his opponent's wrist, attacks with a knife hand strike to the head or face. Dropping the knife hand onto his opponent's arm, Bruce applies palm heel pressure to the attacking elbow and drives his knee home to his opponent's upper arm.

Pulling the assailant down, Bruce executes a further knife hand blow to the back of the neck followed by a blow with the raised knee to the man's face.

BRUCE LEE IN ACTION

swirling speed and grace left them at a loss for words - insufficient phrases like "balletic grace" were bandied about, but soon forgotten. The problem was that martial arts films had been terribly neglected in the West until Bruce Lee burst like an avenging angel onto the scene. The East had had more than its fair share of great Kung Fu films, and was consequently prepared for Lee's genius - compare this review from the *Singapore Sunday Times* with any of the reviews quoted earlier:

"Bruce Lee, Mandarin master of the kiss, karate, and kicks, is back again with a new film with earning power - RETURN OF THE DRAGON."

"There is nothing old hat about the new-style Bruce. He is the symbol of all that is modern in the best tradition of the screen's action heroes.

"As such he is custom-built for the film, which provides another delightful study of Chinese martial arts mixed with karate and lightning kicks."

No bigotry there, no bad jokes or crass moralism at Lee's expense. It is not a great review, but in its simple appreciation of Bruce Lee's magnetic drawing power and understanding of the modern cinema, it puts the pretentious arguments and false judgements of so many western critics to shame.

With so little actual understanding of what Lee was doing, many western critics concentrated their assessments of him purely on the blood and gore that they claimed to dislike, with comments such as, "When nobody is actually dying horribly he is fascinating to watch, a slant-eyed Nureyev of the deadly flashing foot," and, "The combatants move as if they're in a ballet, but they strike to maim or kill. Fists and feet fly, bodies whirl through the air, and there's no shortage of blood. For sheer skill and raw violence, the fights make the average Western set-to seem pretty tame".

This almost grudging appreciation of Lee and his co-stars' brilliant action sequences, with the constant references to "ballet," marks the beginning of western acceptance of Lee on his own terms.

At first the acceptance was reluctant, but the relish with which some writers describe the Little Dragon in action indicate that there's more genuine interest been excited than the cool critic is prepared to admit to. Take this supposedly "intellectual" assessment of Bruce Lee's films from a small British highbrow weekly, *The Spectator*:

"The hero, like a diminutive Samson with the jawbone of an ass, mows his way through countless identical opponents, using a mixture of Judo, Karate chops, Jujitsu and strange salutatory feats which involve somersaulting in mid-air and kicking the victim in the groin with the sole of the foot, all to the accompaniment of sudden sharp cries like a violated parrot, which is apparently to do with correct breathing techniques. Leaving grunting, squirming and expiring novitiates of the martial arts in his wake, the hero eventually comes eyebrow to eyebrow with the Master, upon whom he has several good reasons for revenge, and there begins a protean struggle with hands, legs and bamboo sticks, until the Master, battered and broken, blood pouring from his nose and mouth, sinks to his knees, and the hero administers the coup de grace."

Reluctant as he is to admit it, that writer has certainly got the message!

One of the most disturbing aspects of the press coverage of Lee's films, particularly in the early days, was their constant refusal to check the (quite easily available) facts against their writings. No film star so great can ever have been the subject of so much misinformation so often. A common item was that "He died of internal haemorrhages caused by

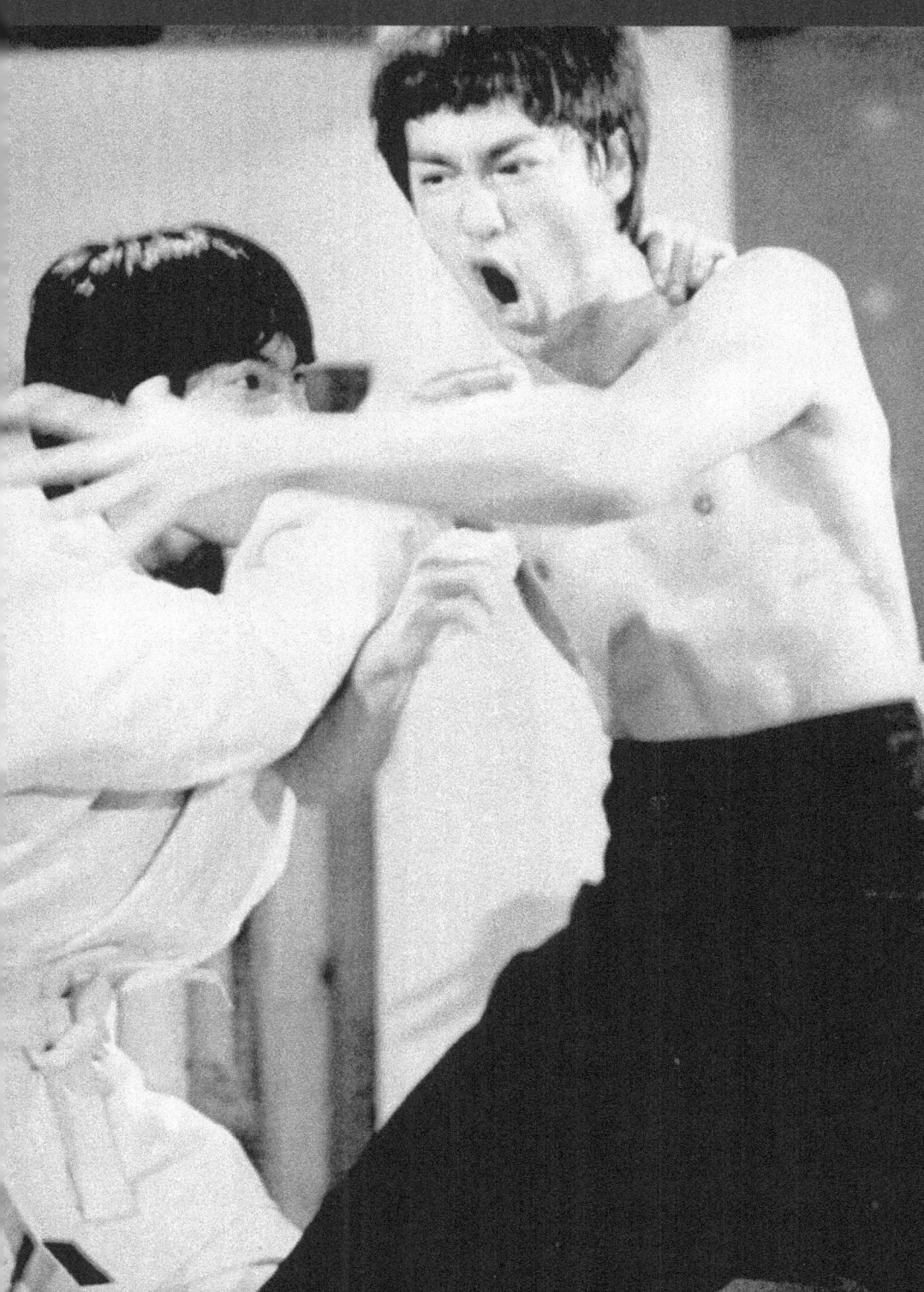

fight scenes in his films." This particular fiction, echoed by papers all over the world, was obviously thought up by somebody with a romantic turn of mind immediately after Lee's tragic death, and it has since been completely disproved.

And take this collection of supposition and simple untruths from a movie magazine, of all places, *Films Illustrated* in December 1973: "When Bruce Lee died in Hong Kong earlier this year, he was in the middle of directing his first film, *Return of the Dragon*, co-starring

BRUCE LEE IN ACTION

Having decimated the Big Boss' henchmen, Bruce Lee (in the photograph demonstrating his famous flying side kick) comes to his climatic fight with the Big Boss himself.

In the initial combat, the Big Boss realises he is outmatched by Lee who drives his opponent back with a series of flying kicks and round-house kicks.

Sensing defeat, he seizes the nearest weapon to hand, in this case a dagger, with which he inflicts several terrible wounds on Lee before being finally overcome. In a half crazed blood lust, Lee clubs his opponent to death with his fists before finally coming back to his senses as the police arrive.

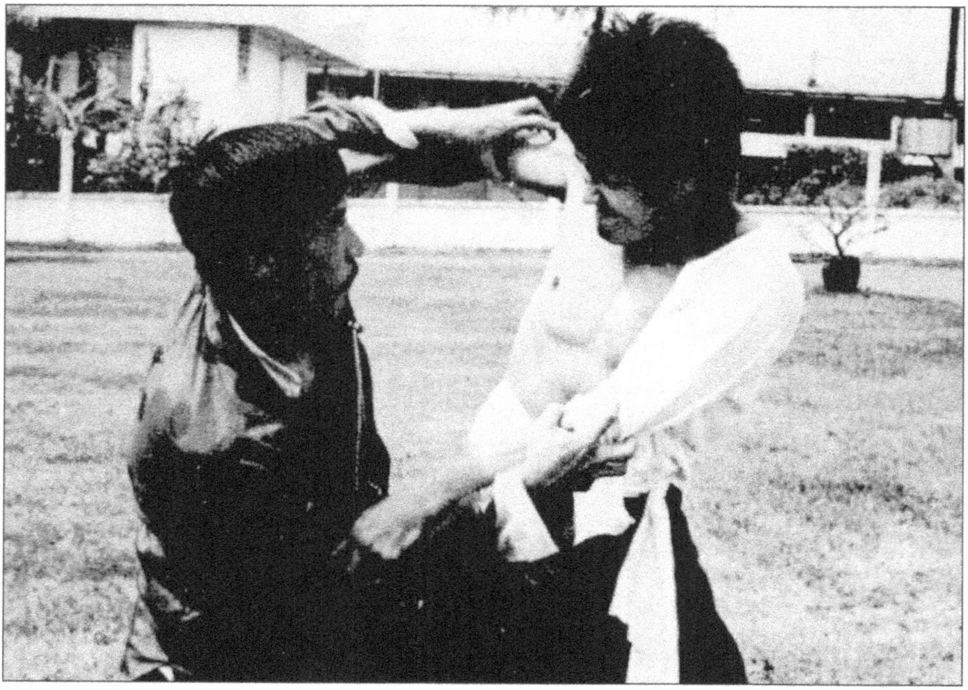

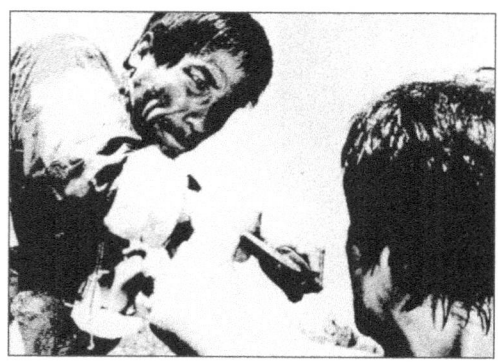

BRUCE LEE IN ACTION

George Lazenby... he was taught the principles of Kung Fu by his father, a star of Chinese opera..." Just to show that the old errors are the best: "The martial arts he performed so brilliantly were to cause his death by internal haemorrhage... as a teenager he appeared in several Chinese films and made his first screen appearance in San Francisco at the age of three months." The writer adds that Lee got a Masters Degree in Philosophy at Washington University, when in fact he dropped out to perfect the martial arts that he loved.

It is hardly possible to imagine a western star of Lee's stature being on the receiving end of so much misinformation and bad research. Not all of the mistakes can be blamed entirely on the critics, however. The changes of title caused endless confusion from one side of the Atlantic to the other. The fact that *The Big Boss* (British title) was called *Fists of Fury* in America, and *Fist of Fury* (British title) renamed *The Chinese Connection* for the States, led a reporter in a major London newspaper to write: "*The Big Boss* broke all box-office records in Hong Kong. *Fists of Fury* followed, then Lee expanded his talents by writing and directing his third feature film. *The Chinese Connection*."

Perhaps it was fortunate that Lee had sufficient faith in himself to ride the storm of criticism, lies, misunderstanding and unfounded rumours that accompanied his rise to fame. A lesser man might have been broken by it all, and rushed off to seek shelter - but not Lee. The essence of his powerful ambition and supreme faith in his own genius was uncovered in a note, written to himself in the late 1960s, hidden, and later discovered by his wife Linda. It reads: "I, Bruce Lee, will be the highest paid Oriental superstar in the United States. In return I will give the most exciting performances and render the best of quality in the capacity of an actor. Starting 1970, I will achieve world fame and from then onward till the end of 1980 I will have in my possession $10,000,000. I will live the way I please and achieve inner harmony and happiness."

Not all the bad reviews in the world could shake that resolve! Perhaps it is sad, though, that Lee was not alive to taste the full sweet flavour of the accolades that the western press came to bestow on him in the years after his death. The obituaries were surely a turning point in the press's attitude towards the greatest martial artist of all time, suddenly it was realised that we had been on the same planet as a genius, and that many had reviled him for it. Amends were made. "Bruce Lee," wrote one western critic, typically, "thou shouldst be alive at this hour. Because Hollywood producers are now scouring the Orient for your replacement."

Another obituarist made the following analogy: "The irrepressible Mr Dean Martin was once heard to remark of fellow Clan member Frank Sinatra: "Some people have got it and some haven't. Frank's got it, had it and even played peaknuckle with it."

"The same might be said of Bruce Lee, whose knowledge and brilliant adaptation of the martial arts made him a legend in his own time."

But perhaps the most touching last word came in a rare magazine article from the famous American folksinger, Phil Ochs, mourning the tragic death of the Little Dragon. "Perhaps he was taken," wrote Ochs, "because he had stolen too much of their fire, and the Gods were jealous."

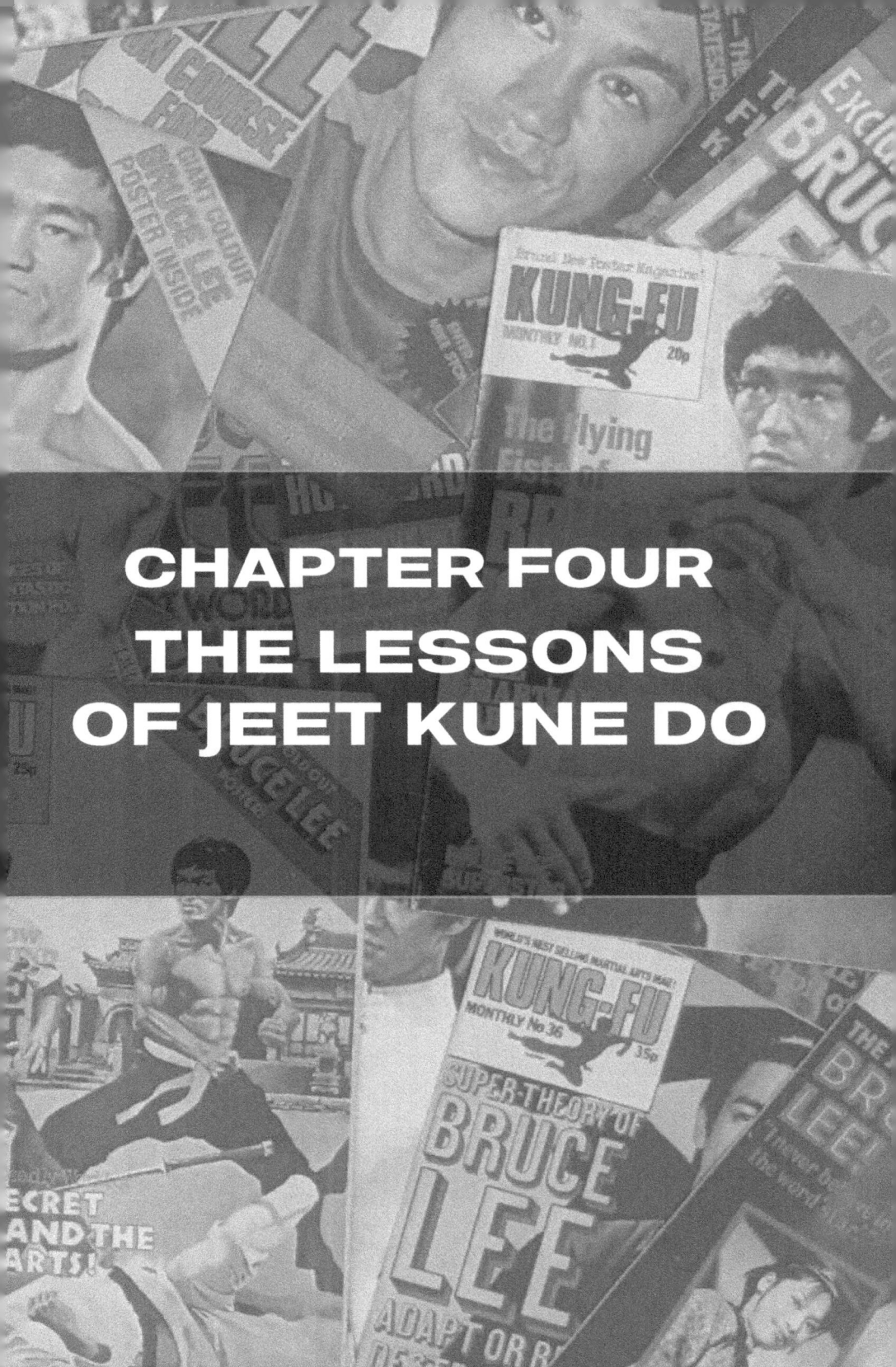

CHAPTER FOUR
THE LESSONS OF JEET KUNE DO

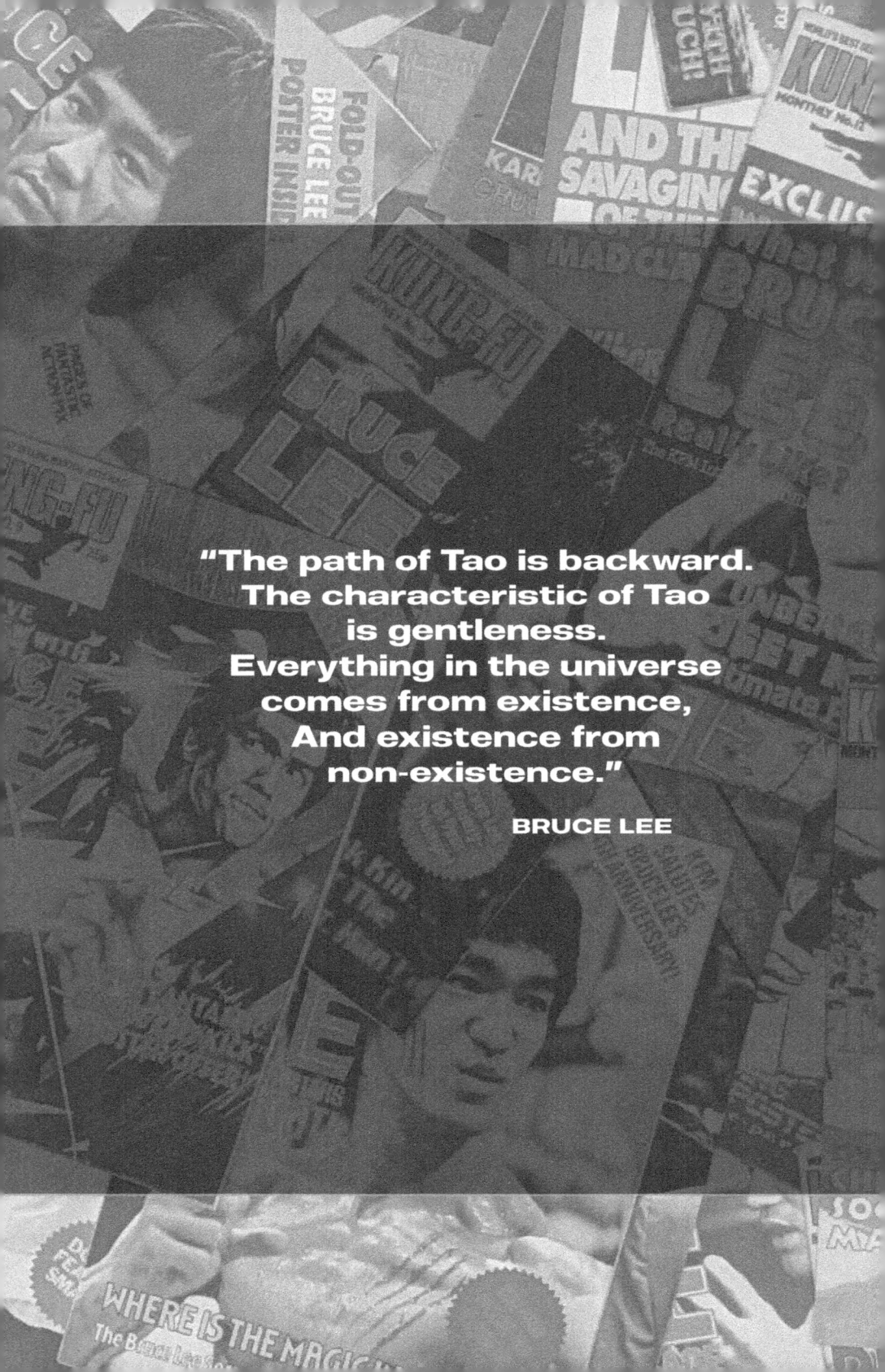

"The path of Tao is backward.
The characteristic of Tao
is gentleness.
Everything in the universe
comes from existence,
And existence from
non-existence."

BRUCE LEE

BRUCE LEE IN ACTION

BRUCE LEE LIVES! In the months following his terrible, untimely death in Hong Kong, this was the cry that echoed round the world. From the Hollywood stars who had befriended and learnt from the Master, to the martial artists from China to California who had accepted him in his own time as the greatest of their kind; from his humblest fan in downtown Kowloon to the biggest studio executive at Warner Brothers - people who had seen or known Bruce Lee were well aware that his legacy would never die.

It was a legacy of many parts. In the world of cinema, Lee had in his short time opened the door to success, and rammed in a wedge that will allow Orientals of talent to stride through and be recognised - a far cry from the time when the best part that any talented Oriental could expect from Hollywood was that of Charlie Chan's *Number One Son*! - "That's what Chinese actors do for a living in Hollywood, isn't it?" Lee once commented with typical sharp irony. "Charlie himself is always played by a round-eye wearing six pounds of make-up."

No more. And in the world of the martial arts, Lee has appeared like a cleansing shower. His acknowledged (indeed, unquestioned) superiority as a martial artist made it difficult, to say the least, for any rival to challenge his theories - for then he must, perforce, challenge Bruce Lee, and that was not an act to be undertaken lightly! It is a tribute to the lasting impression that Lee made on the martial arts that his opponents were unable, after his death, to discredit the man and his theories. Stories turned into legends, and Stirling Silliphant tells of one in particular.

"There were a couple of stuntmen - big tough Caucasian cats - assigned to the movie who were very sceptical about Bruce. They saw this 135-pound Chinese who, when he didn't want to look tough, could maintain a very low profile."

Throughout the day's filming, it became obvious that the stuntmen doubted Lee's ability to choreograph their fight scenes, and were developing running, sarcastic jokes about his size and colour. So Silliphant suggested, to loud guffaws, that Lee demonstrate a few of his skills on the stuntmen. Lee handed an airshield to them.

"One of you guys," he said quietly, "hold this shield. I'm going to give it a little kick. But I suggest you brace yourself first. I kick pretty hard."

With exaggerated fear, the stuntman took the airshield and stood holding it at the edge of the swimming pool. Bruce Lee stood in front of him, about a yard away, and while the stuntman was waiting for him to back off and take a run-up, there was a swish of air, followed by a mighty THWACK, and the stuntman was sailing backwards into the pool.

"That guy", says Silliphant, "came up a Christian! From that moment on, he would have killed for Bruce." His friend, however, was not totally convinced. He wanted to try squatting by the pool, bracing himself for the blow. Again, swish, THWACK, splash! Lee had no further trouble on that set!

Lee was a messiah of the martial arts, in the real sense of the word. His disciples became many in his lifetime. Men like Danny Inosanto - great fighters in their own right - chose to dedicate their time to furthering the philosophy of Bruce Lee. Inosanto still talks of him as the Master: "He could get you emotionally involved. He didn't like to teach more than three students. In fact, in all his teachings, he never taught more than six students at any one time. I think he felt that teaching could not take place if you had more than six students, that you would be drilling like a Karate class, and he didn't want that. He wanted me to carry on the art in the same manner. He said, 'Only six students, Dan.' "

In this sequence, Bruce Lee enters the Japanese Karate school in Shanghai after they have insulted his dead teacher, and proceeds to give them all a lesson in the martial arts!
Single handedly, he defeats the entire body of students with a dazzling display of Kung Fu before disposing of the two main 'heavies' with equal despatch.
Seeing his students cowering before Lee's rage, the head teacher decides to enter the fray himself and teach this upstart a lesson, although, to his surprise, it is Bruce Lee who does the teaching!

These photographs also show the notorious sequence where Lee enters the rival Karate school again at a later date after they have brutally massacred his friends and destroyed the Kung Fu school.

Finding his way to the owner of the school barred by the head teacher, Lee once again demonstrates the superiority of his own style of Kung Fu over Karate. Totally outclassed, the Japanese seizes a large samurai sword with which he attacks. Lee kicks the sword from his hand, and as it sails into the air, pulls his opponent down so the descending sword drives through the teacher's back. Not content with this, Lee finished the fight with a bone-breaking punch to the already mortally wounded man's head.

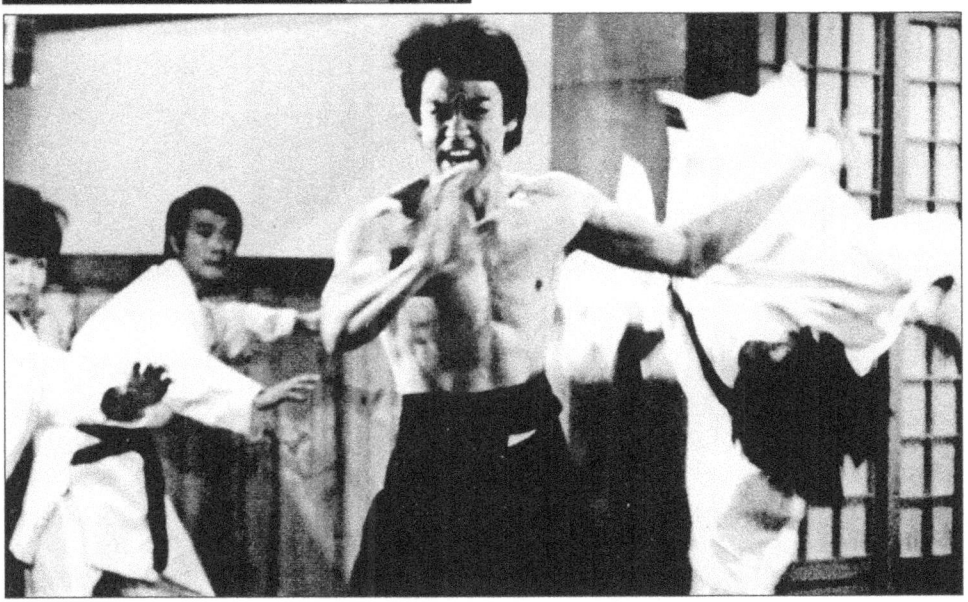

The lessons of Bruce Lee hung around the basic tenets of self-realisation, of each pupil developing according to his or her ability and needs. "I can give you the tools," he once told James Coburn, "but you must develop your own way of using them."

"Look on any tool as an art," he expounded. "Remember, for a single tool to be a masterpiece, it must have totality, speed, agility, power, flexibility, and accuracy. Until you have the ability to move your body and adapt to whatever the object happens to be in front of you, as well as punch and kick from any angle, you still haven't gotten your total efficiency."

Speed, agility, power, flexibility, accuracy - perhaps the greatest of these was flexibility. Bruce Lee's philosophy revolved around the throwing away of false convention, of tradition that had been in practice for so long that most people had forgotten why or how to use it. Lee insisted on the right to draw from any and every martial arts form, without being restricted to or by the semi-religions that had grown up around them. In his later years he realised, just in time, the possibility of Jeet Kune Do becoming just such a strict, inflexible form - against all its real philosophy. He saw the possibility of some bright lad in Hong Kong in years to come being told: "This is the way that you will fight, these are the katas that you will perform, that is the philosophy according to which you will lead your life."

Such a concept would have made Lee shudder, and he did his utmost to ensure that it would never be used under his name. "You must accept the fact," he told the world, "that there is no help but self-help. For the same reason, I cannot tell you how to 'gain' freedom, since freedom exists within you. I cannot tell you how to 'gain' self-knowledge. While I can tell you what not to do, I cannot tell you what you should do, since that would be confining you to a particular approach. Formulas can only inhibit freedom, externally dictated prescriptions only squelch creativity and assure mediocrity."

"Bear in mind that the freedom that accrues from self-knowledge cannot be acquired through strict adherence to a formula; we do not suddenly *become* free, we simply *are* free."

The world has been left more of Bruce Lee than it could reasonably hope for. We have the thousand faces of Lee the actor, we have the twinkle of his eye and the slow, shy smile immortalised on thousands of feet of film. We have the fighting fury of the greatest martial artist of our time, still being shown, week in and week out, at cinemas all over the world. And we have been left the heritage of Jeet Kune Do. Not a style and much, much more than a fighting technique - it is a philosophy for life.

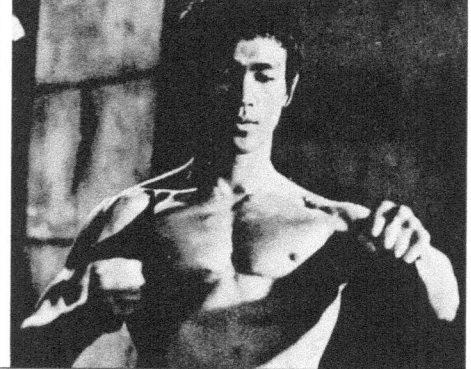

As all Bruce Lee afficionados will probably agree, of all his screen fights, this is probably Bruce's greatest.
In thrilling edge-of-the-seat combat, Bruce Lee comes face-to-face with Chuck Norris, three times world Karate champion, who plays an assassin who has been hired by the syndicate boss to remove the Little Dragon.
In the climax of this memorable piece of cinema, both men confront each other in Rome's famous Colossium. Recognising in each other an opponent of fearsome ability, Lee and Norris begin a rhythm of warm-up calisthenics to raise their

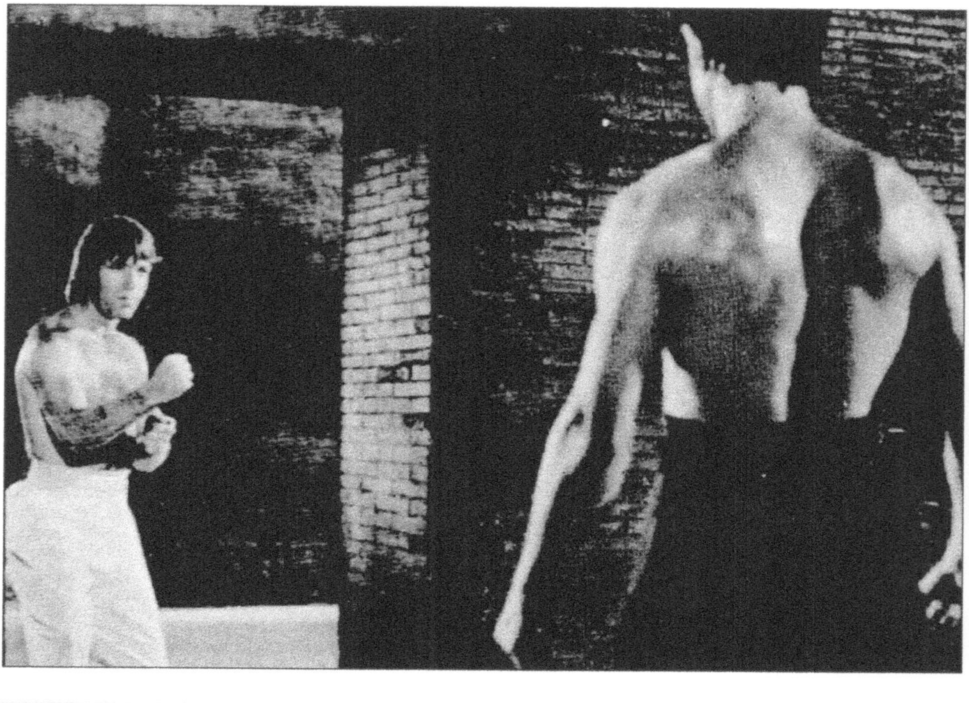

BRUCE LEE IN ACTION

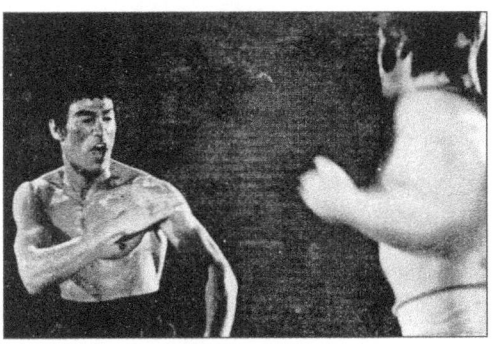

body temperatures and loosen up the muscles and tendons to peak efficiency.
Finally, by unspoken agreement, both men face each other in a large chamber overlooking the vast arena where gladiators of old once fought to the death. A fitting location for such an epic confrontation.
The ensuing fight is divided into two phases. In the first, it takes a more rigid form, both men conforming to the traditional attack and defense patterns of the classical Martial Arts In this, Bruce finds himself mainly on the receiving end, and decides abruptly to change his tactics to a more fluid and flexible form of fighting, in fact his own Jeet Kune Do!
From near defeat at Chuck Norris' hands, Bruce finds himself suddenly with the upper hand. Norris' rigid and traditional training cannot cope with the sudden change of pace and style. Using a combination of bone breaking punches and masterfully executed side and roundhouse kicks, Bruce Lee pounds the black belt champion to a standstill.
The climax of the fight comes when, Lee, recognising and acknowledging the courage of

his opponent, whose leg he has just broken, refuses to go on.
However, Norris, driven on by his pride, will not give up, and lunges at Lee for one last desperate attack. Catching him in a headlock, Lee breaks his neck.
With immense sadness, Lee pays his opponent silent homage, and covers the body with his suit before striding from the arena.

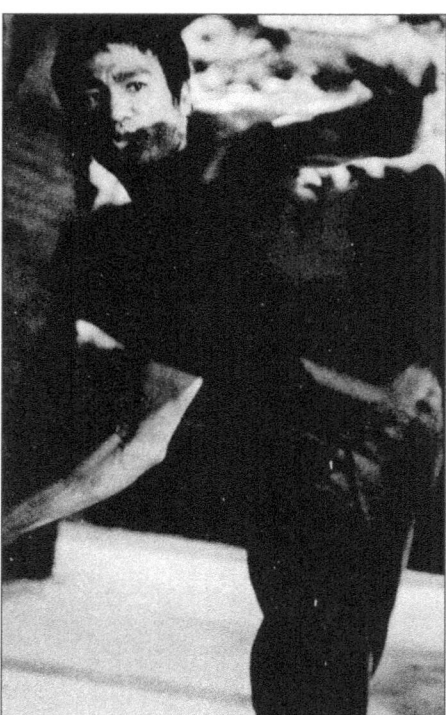

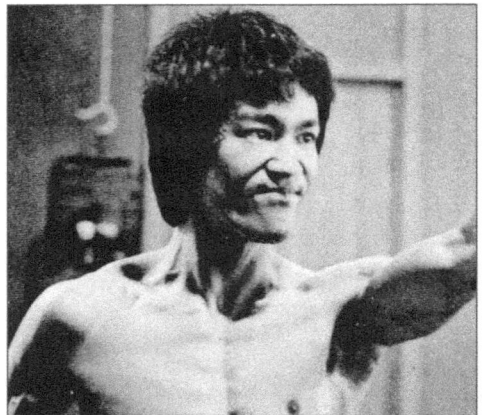

These photographs show the famous scene in Enter the Dragon, where Bruce Lee performs a routine of spectacular calisthenics or warming up exercises in his room prior to the first day of the martial arts tournament.
Bruce practices his own familiar style of punching. Note the incredible muscular tension in his arms, body and neck as he performs a left handed thrust.
It is during a series of kicks that Bruce is disturbed by Oharra. Holding his foot at chest height in the completion of a side kick, Bruce orders him to leave.

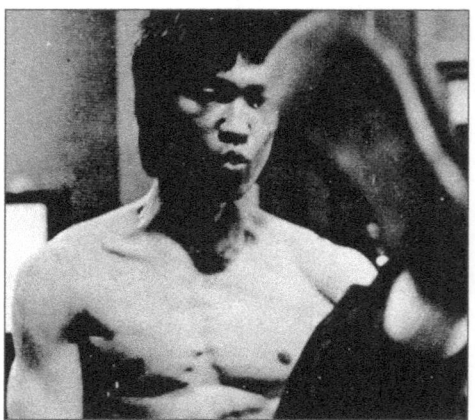

BRUCE LEE IN ACTION

The first of several memorable battles from *Enter the Dragon*, Bruce Lee here is shown in his confrontation with Han's henchman Oharra (Bob Wall) who we have earlier seen as being responsible for the death of Bruce's sister (Angela Mao).

In the opening sequence of the fight, one of the eliminating matches in Han's tournament, Bruce Lee brutally humiliates Oharra with his superior speed and style. With Oharra at his feet, Lee raises a questioning eyebrow at Han. In a blind rage, Oharra seizes Bruce's ankle to throw him over backwards.

Bruce Lee responds by going with the throw and turning a full somersault in mid air, delivering a right-handed kick to Oharra's face before landing on his feet on completion of the throw.

In the last few photograph, Oharra again tries desperately to injure his tormentor, and is shown here attacking with a flying side-kick. Bruce responds by dropping onto his back as shown causing not only the kick to miss, but O'Hara to land painfully onto his outstretched leg!

Blinded with rage and humiliation, and now determined to remove Lee at any cost, O'Hara moves forward in a murderous attack armed with broken bottles. In a scene which was cut from the running version of the film, Lee disarms Oharra with an outside hooking roundhouse kick before moving in for the kill. Remembering what happened to his sister, Lee moves into attack with chilling ferocity - a side kick so powerful that it lifts Oharra from the ground and drives his mortally wounded body crashing through the spectators on the outside of the combat arena.

BRUCE LEE IN ACTION

THE KUNG-FU MONTHLY ARCHIVE SERIES

One of Bruce Lee's many best remembered screen battles is that where he meets the arch villain Han in a fight to the death under Han's island fortress. Having been captured, Lee witnesses John Saxon as Roper defeats Bolo, one of Han's massive and awesome henchmen in a mortal struggle. During the ensuing chaos, Han attempts to make him escape. Spotting his prey, Bruce fights his way across the arena until he reaches Han. Avoiding the murderous claws fitted onto his enemies false hand, Lee delivers a backhanded elbow strike to the face. However, before he can attack again, a

BRUCE LEE IN ACTION

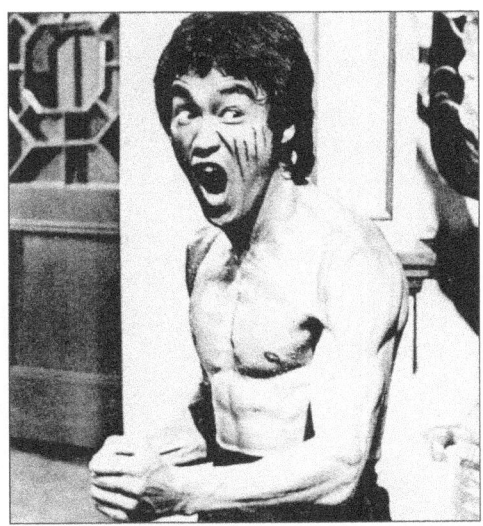
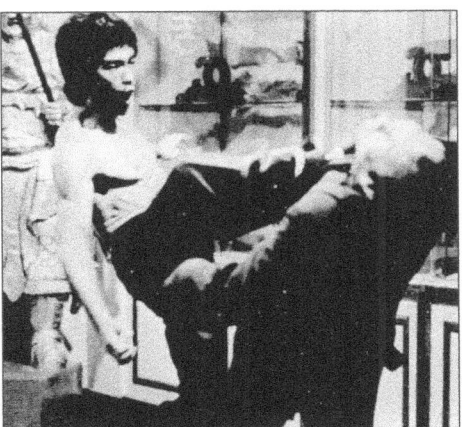

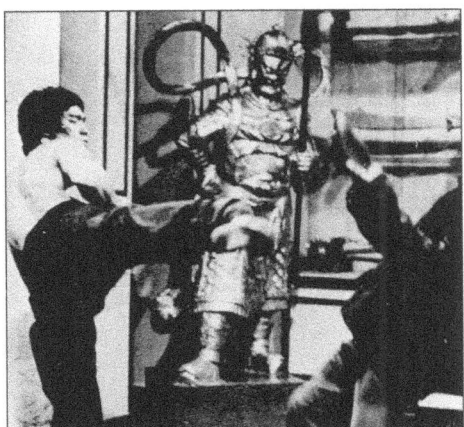

stray punch from the surrounding melee catches him in the face. Turning to flatten this new foe, Bruce unwittingly allows Han to once more melt into the surging mob.

This time however, Lee spots him disappearing through an archway to his underground hideout, and follows in hot pursuit.

Once inside, Han fits a new device to the end of his missing hand - a deadly metal claw fitted with three razor sharp blades a foot long!

As Lee enters, they engage in hand-to-hand combat, a conflict which can only end in death.

The final photograph shows Bruce Lee attacking with a right-handed front kick to the face of his opponent. Wounded several times by the deadly

blades on Han's artificial hand, Lee is spurred on by a savage and elemental fury to become oblivious of his wounds, nothing mattering to him except the death of his enemy. Throwing his opponent to the floor with a sweeping technique, driving him back with combinations of jumping and roundhouse kicks, and finally throwing him to the ground again after trapping his kicking leg in mid-air, Bruce Lee demonstrates his absolute superiority in the fighting arts.

Finally, in a tense climax amidst a hall of mirrors, Lee manages to entrap his opponent, and with a final leaping side kick, throws him back onto the wall where he is impaled on a protruding spear.

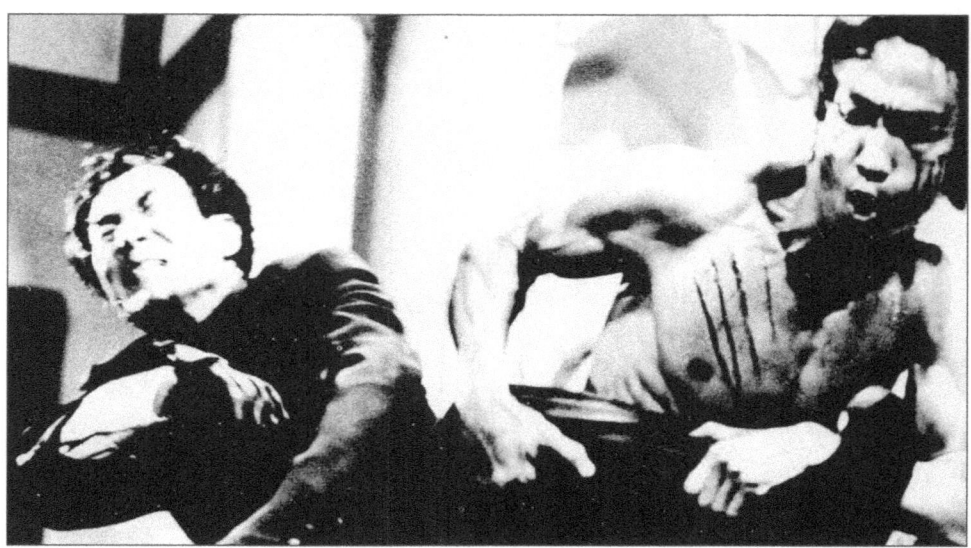

BRUCE LEE IN ACTION

THE KUNG-FU MONTHLY ARCHIVE SERIES

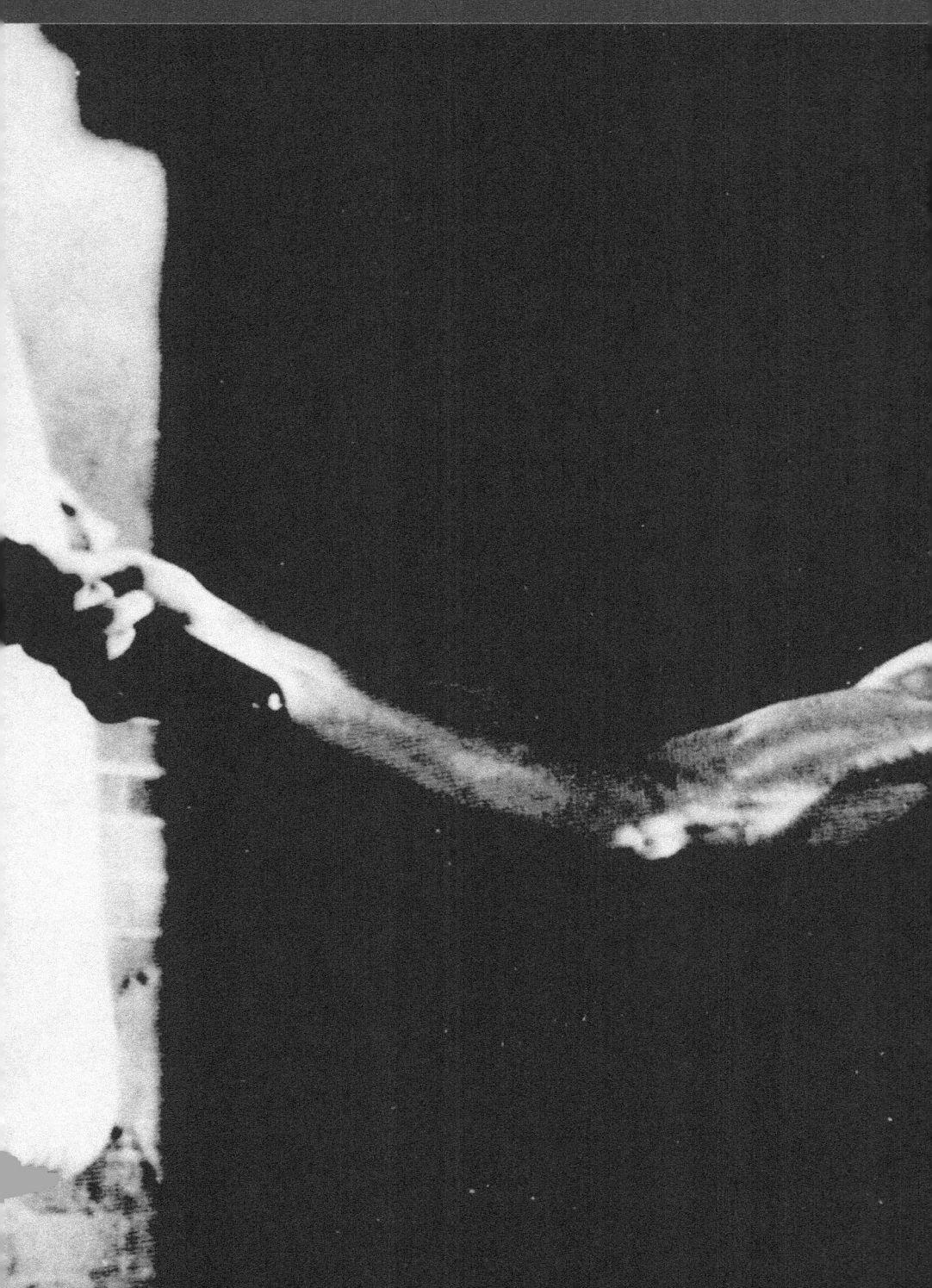

KUNG-FU
20p
THE MARTIAL ART!
GIANT FOLD-OUT
BRUCE LEE
POSTER!
25p
WORLD'S BEST SELLING MARTIAL ARTS MAG!
KUNG-FU
MONTHLY No.36
35p
SUPER-THEORY OF
BRUCE
LEE
GIANT COLOUR
BRUCE LEE
POSTER INSIDE

ALSO BY THE AUTHOR

THE K.F.M. BRUCE LEE SOCIETY

"BEAUTIFULLY CAPTURES THE HEART, SOUL, AND SPIRIT OF THE UNITED KINGDOM'S FLEDGLING BRUCE LEE FANBASE. UNDENIABLY COLLECTIBLE."

- BRUCE LEE REVIEW

"NOT JUST A COMPILATION OF NOSTALGIC NEWSLETTERS, BUT A BRITISH HISTORY GUIDE TO A PERIOD TIME WHEN WESTERN PEOPLE DISCOVERED THE UNIQUE TALENTS OF THE UNDISPUTED KING OF KUNG FU - BRUCE LEE."

- ANDREW J. STATON,
BRITISH JUN FAN JOURNAL

"THANK YOU VERY MUCH FOR YOUR TIME AND EFFORT TO HONOUR PAM FOR HER GREAT WORK AND DEDICATION. I, TOGETHER WITH THE BRUCE LEE FANS WHO KNEW PAM SALUTE YOU!"

- ROBERT LEE

THE **KUNG-FU MONTHLY** BRUCE LEE SECRET SOCIETY BEGAN IN SEPTEMBER 1976, RUNNING FOR 30 ISSUES BEFORE IT'S FINAL ISSUE IN SEPTEMBER 1983. RUN BY THE FORMIDABLE PAM HADDEN, THE BRUCE LEE SECRET SOCIETY FUNCTIONED AS THE SOURCE OF INFORMATION FOR BRUCE LEE FANS IN THE UK AND LATER, THE REST OF THE WORLD. FOR THE FIRST TIME EVER, ALL 30 ISSUES HAVE BEEN PAINSTAKINGLY RE-EDITED AND RE-PRINTED IN THIS BOOK, ALONG WITH UPDATED NOTES AND RETROSPECTIVE STORIES BY THE PEOPLE MOST RESPONSIBLE FOR KEEPING BRUCE LEE'S MEMORY ALIVE - THE FANS.

AVAILABLE FROM **WWW.KUNGFUMONTHLY.UK & AMAZON**

THE WORLD FAMOUS
MARKETPLACE

DON'T FORGET TO VISIT OUR WEBSITE FOR OTHER FANTASTIC ITEMS INCLUDING CLOTHING AND LIMITED EDITION SETS!

BUY ONLINE NOW!

amazon   WHSmith   Waterstones

OR VISIT OUR WEBSITE AT
WWW.KUNGFUMONTHLY.UK

◄ BRUCE LEE KING OF KUNG FU

Written by Felix Dennis & Don Atyeo, Bruce Lee King of Kung Fu is the original and still one of the greatest books on Bruce Lee ever written. Packed with photos and essential information from the immediate year after Lee's tragic death, Bruce Lee King of Kung Fu provides the best of rock-solid backgrounds to the story of the man we all know and love.
170 PAGES

KUNG-FU MONTHLY ► THE POSTER MAGAZINES

Volume One - No. 1 to 25, trade dummy plus an in-depth article on The History of Kung-Fu Monthly 1973 to 1979.
Volume Two - No. 26 to 55 plus interviews with former KFM staff.
Volume Three - No. 56 to 79, double-poster special edition issue plus an in-depth article on The History of Kung-Fu Monthly 1980 to 1984.
540-670 PAGES

THE BOOK OF ► KUNG FU

The Book of Kung Fu was to be Kung-Fu Monthly's special annual issue, but was only published in 1974. Over one-hundred pages, many of them in colour, with a durable soft cover and scores of photographs, illustrations and articles. Don't miss this book! Bruce Lee, Angela Mao, David Carradine, Kung Fu Quiz, Comic Book and more - an incredible publication!
144 PAGES

THE SECRET ART OF ► BRUCE LEE

In 1976, the world took its first look at the now legendary Chester Maydole photographs. Arranged where possible, in 'fast-frame' action sequences, The Secret Art of Bruce Lee shows the founder of Jeet Kune Do, assisted by his friend and student Dan Inosanto, demonstrating the early development state of his art Jeet Kune Do during early days in Los Angeles.
110 PAGES

THE LOST KFM BOOK
FIRST TIME EVER IN THE UK!

◄ **THE WISDOM OF BRUCE LEE**

The Wisdom of Bruce Lee was to be one of the first books in the world to look at Bruce Lee's philosophy on life and martial arts. Mysteriously never released in the UK, The Wisdom of Bruce Lee is finally available to UK Bruce Lee fans after a wait of over forty years.
The full-length version includes a new introduction and interview with author Roger Hutchinson by Jun Fan Journal writer Andrew Staton, while the shorter abridged version is formatted in the style of the original Kung-Fu Monthly books.
70 PAGES / 170 PAGES

◄ **THE UNBEATABLE BRUCE LEE**

The Unbeatable Bruce Lee presents readers with a fighter's view of Bruce Lee the man and Bruce Lee the martial arts master. Beneath the sheer weight of known facts and figures that surround the tragically short life of Hong Kong's number one son, lies a strata of truth that only now is beginning to be picked.
112 PAGES

◄ **BRUCE LEE IN ACTION**

With Bruce Lee in Action, the Editors of Kung-Fu Monthly had compiled another fine addition to their library of Bruce Lee publications. Lavishly illustrated throughout with many previously unseen photographs at the time, this informative book investigates clearly and concisely, the birth and subsequent development of Lee's fighting style Jeet Kune Do, both on and off the screen.
106 PAGES

**THE POWER OF ►
BRUCE LEE**

Bruce Lee was possibly the greatest exponent of the martial arts ever produced. The fact that he was a movie star often clouds his enormous contribution to the field. The Power of Bruce Lee explores many of his revolutionary methods of attack and defence, especially those relating to Jeet Kune Do, Lee's name for his own fighting system
110 PAGES

**WHO KILLED ►
BRUCE LEE?**

Who Killed Bruce Lee? is a study of the pressures and the forces that, on the one hand were to elevate him to the highest plains of stardom and on the other, were to so tragically strike him down before his final fulfilment.
Who Killed Bruce Lee? was one of the first books to delve deep into the newspaper stories of Lee's early death.
108 PAGES

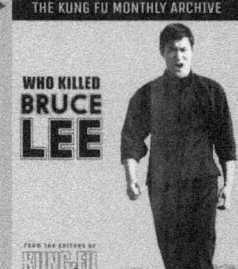

◀ **THE GAME OF DEATH**

This book combines two Kung-Fu Monthly special edition magazines released prior to Golden Harvest's 1978 film. Researched exclusively in Hong Kong, Kung-Fu Monthly reports on Lee's plot for Game of Death, the cast he intended to appear in the film, the scenes already filmed and Lee's hopes and expectations for the success of the project. Incredibly accurate for the time, this publication represents an important part of Bruce Lee fandom in the UK.
XXX PAGES

THE MAGAZINES

WWW.KUNGFUMONTHLY.UK

◀ **THE BEGINNER'S GUIDE TO KUNG FU**

Originally released in 1974, The Beginner's Guide to Kung Fu was the first martial arts book aimed primarily at the Kung Fu Craze generation. The graphic, easy to understand illustrations by Paul Simmons and the carefully conceived step by step instructions made this the perfect book for beginners who wished to take up Kung Fu.
XXX PAGES

▲

THE BRUCE LEE SCRAPBOOK

In 1974, Kung-Fu Monthly issued a Bruce Lee scrapbook in the form of a large A3 magazine, followed by a smaller A4 sized book in 1979. As part of the KFM Archive Series, both scrapbooks have been combined in a new chronological layout with brand new captions, location information and dates by Carl Fox and Jun Fan Journal writer Andrew Staton.
150 PAGES

THE KFM BRUCE LEE SOCIETY ▶

Long before the internet communities we know today, The Bruce Lee Society was the source of information in the United Kingdom for all things Bruce Lee. Now the history of the Bruce Lee Society is finally told in The Bruce Lee Society: A Retrospective Look at Bruce Lee Mania and the Kung Fu Craze of the 1970s. For the first time ever, all thirty issues of The Bruce Lee Society newsletters have been painstakingly re-edited and re-printed in this book, along with updated notes and retrospective stories by the people most responsible for keeping Bruce Lee's memory alive - the fans.
544 PAGES

www.ingramcontent.com/pod-product-compliance
Lightning Source LLC
Chambersburg PA
CBHW041323110526
44591CB00021B/2883